ROOFTOP GARDEN

GINGKO PRESS

FOREWORD

Domestic professional books on roof garden design is relatively few, Overall, relatively too old or too few of the cases make it difficult to grasp the latest development trend around the world for readers. While some other books can not show the roof garden design fully because of the lacking of professional editors, experts, compiled together with design company and so on. Base on those facts, **Hong Kong Architecture Science Press** Editorial Board plans carefully to compile the book *Rooftop Garden* to help flush the teaching material in domestic education for this topic.

After the world wide selection, Editorial Board verified 40 representative projects in this book. Differing from program mode explanations in previous books, it focuses on the excavation of connotation value. Editors show the key points and hot spots of every project for readers. Project analyses show the highlights and features from geography, climate, vegetation, materials, and ecological value. We also invite experts in or outside of China to comment the project combined with realities, and put forward different views for readers' references. In addition, "tips" related with new trends attached to each layout of project, facilitate readers to understand the background, extending learning.

This book with carefully arranged of HD pictures and graceful sentence, lets readers enjoy science education informations, and at the same time makes them feel the charm of roof garden in aesthetics. Hope that this book can become a catalyst for advancing domestic rooftop garden design and construction.

Thanks for all the designer (experts) teams who participated in compiling this book again!

Hong Kong Architecture Science Press
Editorial Board
2013.3

PREFACE

Turn the rooftop into green oasis!

The modern architecture with flat roof-space has provided us with new opportunity to bring the nature back to cities, making them greener and friendlier as well as healthier places to live. These vast lands which were long ago borrowed from the nature, turned into concrete jungles, lost all of its greenery with few exceptions in terms of parks and rare green avenues.

There is so much unused potential around us, just go up to a high-rise building and have a look from there - how many green dots you can spot? But how many empty roofs, smaller or larger space that could be turned into green oasis?

Roof gardens have rather impressive history, although there were very few privileged people who could really afford building these structures. The ancient representation of roof gardens were the Hanging Gardens of Babylon, the vaulted terraces that were lush with overhanging plants and trees in the middle of sun-baked and flat Mesopotamia, built around 600 BC. The Romans were known for their roof gardens in Pompei, Villa of the Mysteries excavations proved and identified the plants that were planted directly on soil in one of its terraces. Imperial city of the Aztecs, Tenochtitlan was also known to have had roof gardens as well as the impressive Mont Saint Michel, emerging from the sea in Normandy, France.

First commercial rooftop gardens in New York are dated from 1882 when the Casino Theatre was built, quickly followed by Madison Square Garden. The absence of air-conditioning guaranteed the success of these spaces as hot summers closed the theatre season indoors and brought the opera, dances and plays to the outdoors. The beginning of 20th century saw huge growth in using the rooftop space – many hotels opened up pleasure gardens on their roofs, office buildings created open-air restaurants and wealthy house-owners used it for enhancing the upscale apartments. It was rather common to use the rooftop for games such as basketball, baseball and tennis, also dances. The not-so-wealthy people also found their own way to creatively use the 'new' and valuable space.

The first gardens on roofs in Europe were born in the 1930s and 1940s. London's Derry and Toms Roof Garden, today known as Kensington Roof Garden was commissioned by a department store that gave the garden its name and covered an area of 1,5 acres (about 6070 m²) with fountains, ponds and bridges, different walks and even a woodland garden. It sits on the top of a 30 m high building. The other better-known roof-garden was designed by Swiss architect Le Corbusier in Marseilles, France. La Cité Radieuse, so-called vertical living for over 1600 people with a communal space on the roof, was completed in 1952. It features a swimming pool, recreation ground and children's nursery.

Today, with all that history and exciting examples, why is there still so much unused potential? Why have we not seen that space, nor dared to do anything with it? There must be multiple reasons, financial, constructional or simply no available information on how to fill these spaces effectively and successfully. True, a rooftop garden needs a wise approach, some detailed research and knowledgeable completion but is not that complicated that one should not consider using that space for its advantage.

Why to create a rooftop garden overall? Gardens in the sky enjoy privileged status for many reasons. They are highly valued as being a limited space where every square metre counts, a potential for different activities, relaxing or just enjoying the beauty of nature, enlarging the indoor-living space. Being higher up and closer to the sky, it offers cleaner, fresh air which may not be a commonplace in a busy city. A space which cuts off the traffic noise, lends beautiful or interesting views, curious perspectives, something you would not see unless you are higher up. Rooftop gardens also enjoy greater privacy. Being in a green haven, in the middle of a bustling city, makes it all more valuable, every tree and every bloom there stands out, every season becomes more apparent with its changes, moods and colours. It is a living organism which you can create and direct the way you wish.

True, these spaces present us with many challenges that you would normally not be concerned about when creating a garden on ground. Weight concerns, structural and safety issues, harsh winds and weather conditions that are quite different, heat or freezing matters, unexpected microclimates and a number of other aspects are to be taken into account. There are some general rules which apply to most of the rooftop gardens in the world, and thanks to fast globalization, there is increasing amount of literature available regarding construction, specifications and planting on roofs. But you should also be ready and know that there are some surprises, good or bad that do not follow these facts and rules of thumb. Just enjoy the process and be prepared for what may come, it is a learning curve for even the best of designers.

This book will first of all, inspire you giving some great ideas what to do with an empty roof-space, whether it is tiny or rather spacious one. It will advise how to create interesting and effective garden rooms, allow different moods, point out which furniture to use, how to approach lighting and sculpture, use creative accessories to a garden's advantage. And of course feature lot of planting which has a final say in every rooftop garden. There are plans, some construction drawings, views and other details, great tips and general information about these spaces. It is a valuable first step towards creating more and more of them, giving you a gentle nudge towards being more open to creative possibilities, things you may not have seen earlier or considered possible. May it lead you into something wonderful, whether it is in a form of an idea, end result, exciting cooperation or help you becoming just a brighter happier person.

Merilen Mentaal
Member of Society of Garden Designers,
Garden Designer
MentaalLandscapes

CONTENTS

Public Leisure

Community Ecology

CONTENTS

Private Rooftop

Ecological Green

PUBLIC
LEISURE

"Star skygarden standing on Marina Bay"

Marina Bay Sands

Landscape Architect: PWP Landscape Architecture
Client: Las Vegas Sands
Location: Singapore
Site Area: 9,941 m²
Photography: Tim Hursley, Timothy Hursley

CLIMATIC CONDITIONS

Singapore belongs to tropical rainforest climate, temperature is hot and humid, the minimum difference in daily and yearly temperature, monthly average temperature 24-27 degrees, annual rainfall is about 2,400 mm, with no typhoon harassment.

PLANTS

Palm, Khaya, Peitophorum, Alstonia

EDITOR'S CHOICE

The super sky garden attracts world's attention by its impressive shape as a ship connecting the top of three volumes. It includes an infinite pool and a spacious viewing platform that offers 360 degree views around downtown Singapore.

Sands Sky Park –the three hotel towers are connected at the top (200 meters/656 feet) by a 9,941 square meter (107,000 square foot) park that brings together a public observatory, jogging paths, gardens, restaurants, lounges, and an infinity swimming pool. This 1.2 hectare (3 acre) tropical oasis is longer than the Eiffel Tower which is tall and large enough to park four-and-a-half A380 jumbo jets. It spans from tower to tower and cantilevers 65 meters (213 feet) beyond to form one of the world's largest public cantilevers. It is 340 meters (1,115 feet) long from the northern tip to the south end. The park's maximum width is 40 meters (131 feet) .The 1,396 square meter (15,026 square foot) swimming pool is the largest outdoor pool at its height and has a 145 meter (475 foot) vanishing edge. The entire park can host up to 3,900 people. Its lush gardens include 250 trees and 650 plants.

PWP worked with the Singapore government, Moshe Safdie, and a team of local landscape architects and horticulturalists as well as engineering, architectural, and business professionals to create the landscape for this project at the entrance to Singapore Bay. It includes a public waterfront promenade, a public rooftop promenade, and a 1,000-meter-long landscaped bridge. The 2.5-acre skypark spans the roofs of three hotel towers on the 57th floor and offers views of downtown Singapore.

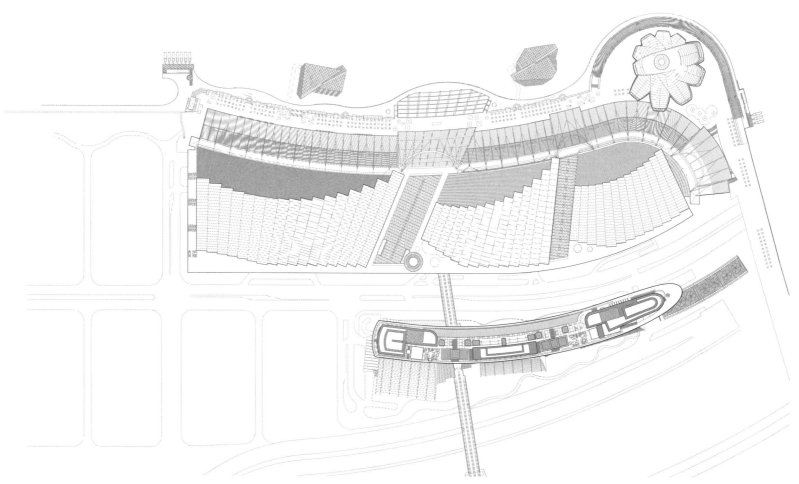

Site Plan

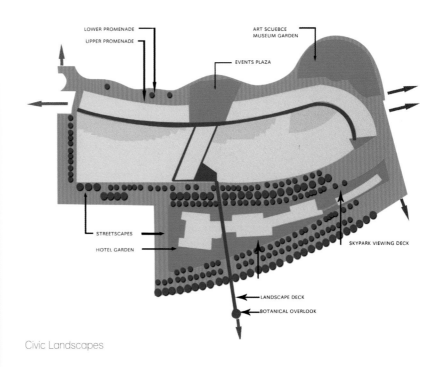

Civic Landscapes

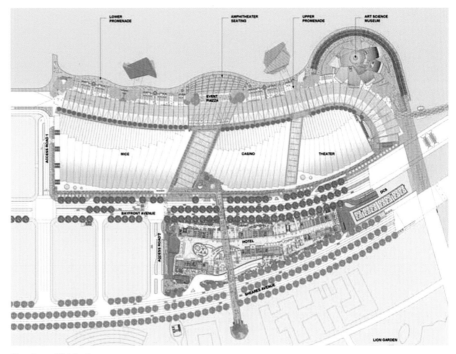

Functions Distribution

Landscape occupies nearly 30 acres at Marina Bay Sands, 75 percent of which is public space. The half-mile-long Waterfront Promenade features a triple allée of Roystonia palms interspersed with informal groupings of large canopy trees such as Khaya, Peltophorum, and Alstonia— that provide both scale and much-needed shade. Permeable pavement systems collect surface drainage and reduce runoff.

The skypark, a surprising garden in the sky, features a swimming pool with an infinity edge, garden rooms of lush plantings and mature trees, a public viewing deck, and three restaurants. PWP conceived of an early tree-procurement strategy as well as a temporary-nursery plan that permitted plants to be sourced overseas from many locales and facilitated the installation of large quantities of mature trees with a high success rate.

COMMENT

Combining the architecture as a whole, the roof garden has won a reputation of worldwide classic in high-rise garden design, while creating a new Singapore attraction for the public.

Corlee

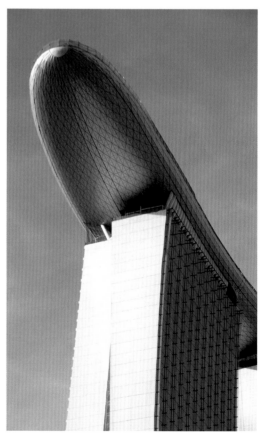

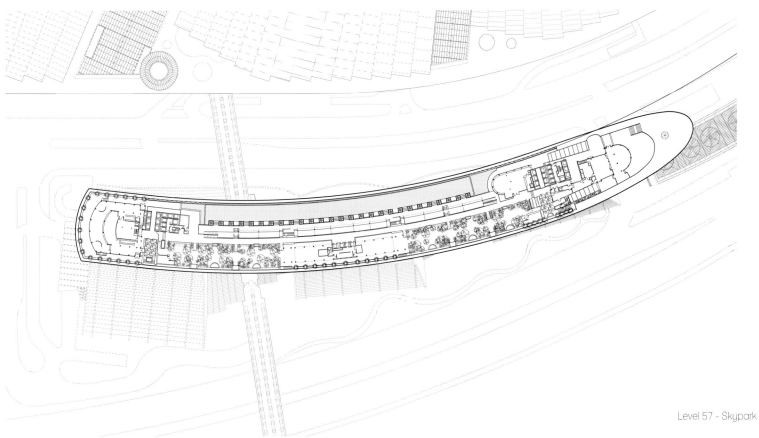

Level 57 - Skypark

"Create the perfect fusion of working, relaxation and sightseeing."

900 North Michigan Avenue

Landscape Architect: Hoerr Schaudt Landscape Architects
Client: JMB Realty
Location: Chicago, Illinois, USA
Site Area: 1,486.4 m²(Garage), 1,291.4 m²(Residences), 641 m²(Office)
Cost: $ 500,000(Garage), $ 540,000(Residences), $ 600,000(Office)
Photography: Linda Oyama Bryan, Scott Shigley

CLIMATIC CONDITIONS

Chicago is also known as the "Windy City". It belongs to temperate continental climate with distinct seasons. Subjected to the influence of Lake Michigan, it has great temperature different between winter and summer with sufficient rainfall.

PLANTS

stonecrop, sedum, chive, feather reed grass, serviceberry, boxwood, cotoneaster

EDITOR'S CHOICE

The roof of the office building is like an abstract painting changed in four seasons; the roof of the residential building reduces loading by giving up hard landscape and vertical greening on parking area helps to clear air pollution to meet the standards of Chicago Parking Regulation. In addition, the façade of the parking area facing the street has achieved more than 50% greening rate.

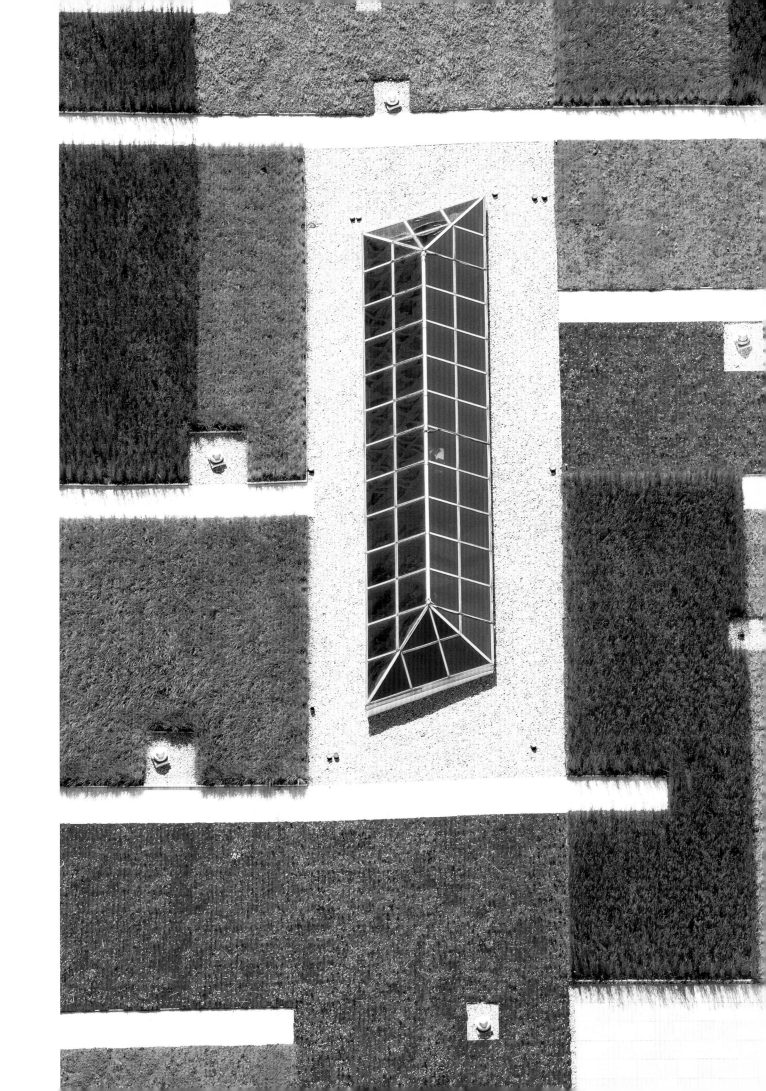

The mixed-use complex at 900 North Michigan Avenue is comprised of a four-star hotel, luxury condominiums, office tenants, a parking garage, and high-end retail along one of the city's most prestigious corridors. The building is a significant presence, whether viewed from the ground level or through the thousands of windows that look down on it from surrounding towers. Green space is a prized amenity in this densely-packed neighborhood, which relies on proximity to lakefront parks for most of its recreation needs. Views from high-rises are spectacular, but few offer views of green.

RUSH / WALTON PARKING GARAGE

900 N. MICHIGAN AVENUE

MICHIGAN AVENUE

WEST DELAWARE STREET

Site Plan

0'   50'   100'

Three green roof projects at one of the most upscale mixed-use complexes on Michigan Avenue challenge status quo assumptions about what can be expected both from a city view and from green roofs. The projects, completed by Hoerr Schaudt over a period of six years for a single client, share a common aesthetic but are designed to respond to the varied needs of three different end users: one for the luxury residences, one on the adjacent parking garage, and the last on the east side of the building for office tenants. They are boldly graphic and legible to thousands of people to view them daily.

Though designed for different end users, all three roofs have common design elements. The planting and structural patterns of all three are inspired by aerial views of the Midwest's agricultural landscape. All utilize modular green roof systems with modified planting mixes that incorporate grasses and perennials for the majority of the planted areas. Seasonal colors and views from above, which are the primary way most people experience the roofs, are extremely important considerations. The height varieties in the plant material create an unfolding, multidimensional experience from within the garden, and create shadow and depth throughout the seasons when viewed from above. Each is designed to be a tapestry of ever-changing pattern and color. On each roof, Hoerr Schaudt pushed for the design to occupy as much space as possible and for it to include as much vegetation as possible. Lastly, all the roof designs response to the available structural capacities on the existing building, which restrict how much (if any) of the roof could be occupied.

Residences

Hoerr Schaudt designs a green roof where residents could entertain or relax in a garden-like environment. Weight restrictions limit hardscape-intensive design solutions. Hoerr Schaudt utilizes a standard green roof tray system – in 4- and 8-inch depths – and raises it atop polystyrene insulation to level the field of trays with an entertainment deck and boardwalk. Within the deck, two custom-designed pergolas by Hoerr Schaudt frame views of the skyline and provide a sense of intimacy in what could have been a daunting exposure, given the looming skyscrapers. Night lighting adheres to the dark sky criteria set forth in current LEED guidelines. At the entrance to the roof, deeper planters hold enough soil to support trees and shrubs.

Parking Garage

The City of Chicago Parking Garage ordinance requires certain parking garages to 'green' up to 50 percent of its façade that is open to the street. Hoerr Schaudt was retained by the client to develop a vertical greening solution. However, given the location of this deck and its limited access to sunlight, we suggested an alter-native: utilize the unused 'fifth façade' of the building to fulfill the zoning requirement.

Because the roof was inaccessible for parking – there was office space at the top level of the garage and the roof was underutilized – using the space for a 16,000 square foot green roof creatively met city goals for urban greening while reducing stormwater runoff and helping to reduce the heat island effect.

Aesthetically, the design of this roof is sympathetic to the roof at the Residences. Five planting mixes are organized in an irregular grid pattern and include Stonecrop, sedum, chive, and feather reed grass. To most of the people viewing the residential and garage green roofs on a daily basis from above, they appear as a unit.

Offices

This 6,900 square foot roof garden is designed to be experienced on two levels. From above, viewers experience the roof as an abstract composition that changes with the seasons. From within, visitors are immersed in a multi-level garden that offers a dynamic juxtaposition to the sky, lake, and surrounding skyline. Most of the plantings are modular 4" and 6" trays with a modified mix of plantings. A raised planter that runs along the windows of the 9th floor allows for more soil depth, and is planted with serviceberry, boxwood, and cotoneaster. A stone terrace surrounded by granite benches creates an inviting place for people to meet or relax. Due to the height of surrounding buildings, this roof gets little sun except for a few hours in the morning. Plant mixes of are designed to accommodate less direct sunlight.

TIPS

Development of Roof Greeny

For various environmental problems caused by the rapid development of urbanization, many metropolitans, such as Tokyo, Beijing, Shenzhen, Hangzhou, etc. have introduced related policies to lead rooftop greening development. Assumes that if there are 30% green roofs in Beijing's 69.79 million sqm built-up areas, which equals 27 new built parks in Beijing downtown. It will add 369.8 sqm greening areas that attribute to keep 192.45 tons of dusts and reduce 3.95 tons of SO_2, which significantly improve the air quality.

Farmerson

COMMENT

The designer acting as professional experts has solved a serious of problems for site limited by an integrated design. The inevitable problem of "planarity" on the roof is perfectly done by texture of plants and seasonal changes in a modernist approach.

"Planting grasses, setting stones, creating a painting."

Washington Mutual Center Roof

Landscape Architect: Phillips Farevaag Smallenberg
Client: Washington Mutual Bank
Location: Seattle, Washington, USA
Photography: George White Photography, Lara Swimmer Photography, Joseph Fry (PFS)

CLIMATIC CONDITIONS

Washington has four distinct seasons, mild climate, which is typical subtropical moist climate.

EDITOR'S CHOICE

"Money Garden" and "glass bead abacus screen wall" stand for the Bank and its history, while two-thirds green areas make it to be one of the largest Seattle roof garden.

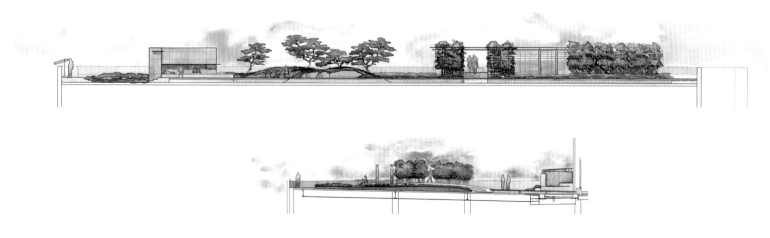

Side View

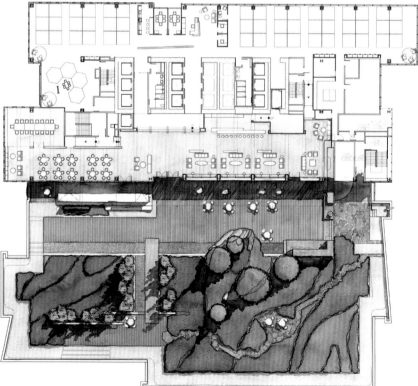

The landscape architect for the project develops design concepts for the roof 17th floor roof deck in close collaboration with the architect and project engineers. Curtain walls and seats at the building edge further connect the garden to the interior lounge, creating a seamless indoor-outdoor experience. Key collaborative efforts include working with architects, interior designers, and structural engineers to develop an outdoor fireplace, boulder outcroppings, and windscreens into a fully integrated landscape and building design.

Site Plan

As a result the garden has already become the most vital social and event space for the client's central downtown campus. Planting, pathways, and wood decking were designed to symbolically represent the diverse landscapes of Washington State. As almost two-thirds of the deck is planted with predominantly drought-tolerant and native plants, the 17th floor garden has already gained the reputation as one of Seattle's largest green roofs.

An understated feature of the roof garden is how it combines usable public space for human enjoyment with many broader ecological green roof attributes, including urban heat island effect reduction, stormwater retention, and native and drought-tolerant planting. This project demonstrates that sustainable landscape roof design need not be limited to extensive low-maintenance green roofs, but that it can also be practical, social, symbolic, and contemporary.

Two unique features in the garden symbolize the bank and its history: a glass-beaded abacus screen wall is a whimsical and interactive version of an ancient tool of counting, and 'The Change Garden' - a repository for spare change that will be donated to Seattle's charitable organizations - demonstrates the Bank's ongoing role as a leading corporate citizen.

Challenges faced during construction of the project included a short window for installation of roof elements including boulder placement, screen and deck installation, and collaboration with interior finishes. The boulder outcrop was particularly challenging from a weight and handling perspective. Extensive planning to select and mockup the boulder composition off-site resulted in a swift re-assembly on the deck with limited impact on overall building construction schedules, crane time, or other adjacent trade work.

TIPS

Landscape stone
With appropriate forms, colors, qualities and textures will help increase the appreciation the whole project. Elegant or rough, landscape stones offer a wild natural sense for people to enjoy.

Farmerson

COMMENT

Apparently, the glass-beaded abacus screen wall and the Change Garden are aimed to demonstrate the theme of the bank. The essence of the design lies at introducing nature into this artificial garden.

"The scene only be in heaven, or the Paradise falls on earth."

Rooftop Garden of
Hilton Central Pattaya Hotel

Landscape Architect: T.R.O.P terrains+open space
Client: Central Pattana (CPN)
Location: Pattaya Chonburi, Thailand
Site Area: 2,538 m²
Photography: Adam Brozzone, Charkhrit Chartarsa, Pok Kobkongsanti

CLIMATIC CONDITIONS

Chonburi locates in tropical area with a suitable climate in summers, the average temperature is from 21.9 to 35.7 ℃.

PLANTS

crescentia cujete, areca catechu, hymenocallis sp., sansevieria trifasciata, washingtonia filifera, nymphaea spp., etc.

EDITOR'S CHOICE

The designer skillfully avoids the limitations of the site by hidden the rough skylight by grass and reasonably plan or create limited but necessary spaces dotted by finishing and furniture filled with tropical furnishings. What's more, with the infinite pool seemed to overflow to the sky, a relaxing and leisure holiday atmosphere is born.

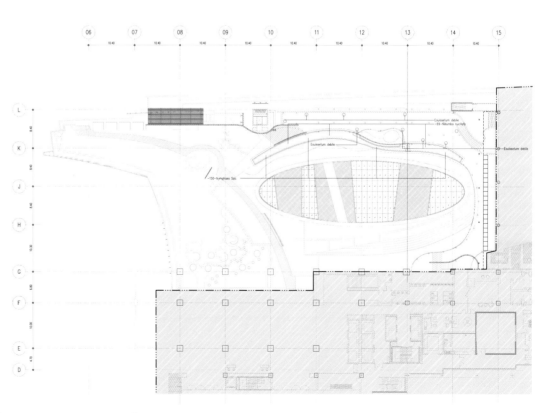

16th (Mezzanine)Shrub Plan

(A) <u>16th. (MEZZANINE) SHRUB PLAN</u>
SCALE   1:250

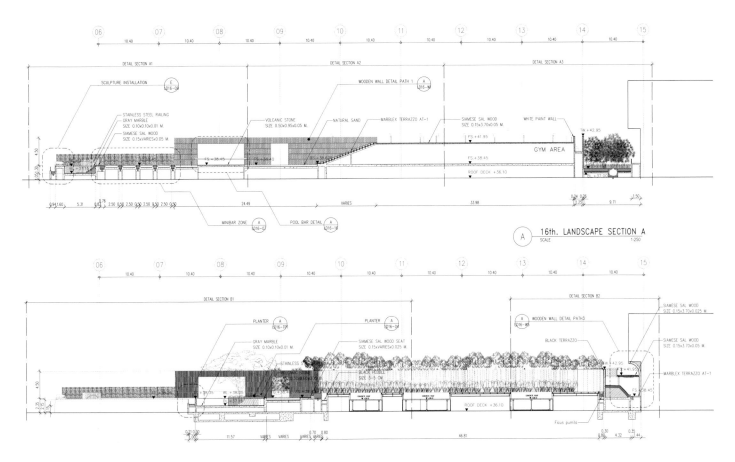

10.40 10.40 10.40 10.40 10.40 10.40 10.40 10.40 10.40

DETAIL SECTION A1   DETAIL SECTION A2   DETAIL SECTION A3

SCULPTURE INSTALLATION

E
1016-08

WOODEN WALL DETAIL PATH 1

A
1016-M

STAINLESS STEEL RAILING
GRAY MARBLE
SIZE 0.10x0.10x0.01 M.

VOLCANIC STONE
SIZE 0.50x0.95x0.05 M.

NATURAL SAND

MARBLEX TERRAZZO AT-1

SIAMESE SAL WOOD
SIZE 0.15x3.70x0.05 M.

WHITE PAINT WALL

SIAMESE SAL WOOD
SIZE 0.15xVARIES x0.05 M.

TW. +42.95

FS. +41.95

GYM AREA

FS. +38.45

ROOF DECK +36.10

BL. +37.00

FS. +38.45   FS. +34.40

4.50

0.50 0.30

0.94 1.60   5.31   0.76   2.50 0.50 0.50 2.50 0.50 2.50 0.50   24.49   VARES   33.98   0.24 0.26   9.71   1.50
0.81   0.25

MINIBAR ZONE
A
1016-07

POOL BAR DETAIL
A
1016-16

A   16th. LANDSCAPE SECTION A
SCALE   1:250

10.40 10.40 10.40 10.40 10.40 10.40 10.40 10.40 10.40

DETAIL SECTION B1   DETAIL SECTION B2

SIAMESE SAL WOOD
SIZE 0.15x3.70x0.025 M.

PLANTER
A
1016-19

PLANTER
A
1016-04

A
1016-M

WOODEN WALL DETAIL PATH3

SIAMESE SAL WOOD
SIZE 0.15x3.70x0.05 M.

GRAY MARBLE
SIZE 0.10x0.10x0.01 M.

SIAMESE SAL WOOD SEAT
SIZE 0.15xVARIES x0.025 M.

BLACK TERRAZZO

MARBLEX TERRAZZO AT-1

STAINLESS S...

BLACK PEBBLE
SIZE 3-5 CM.

TW. +42.95
FS. +41.95

4.50

2.35

FS. +38.35   WL. +38.05   ROOF DECK +36.10   FS. +38.45

2.15   CONCRETE ROOF

Ficus pumila

0.21 0.30   11.57   VARES   VARES   0.70 0.80   46.81   0.30   4.32   0.35
0.00   VARES VARES   0.80   0.44

16th Landscape Section A

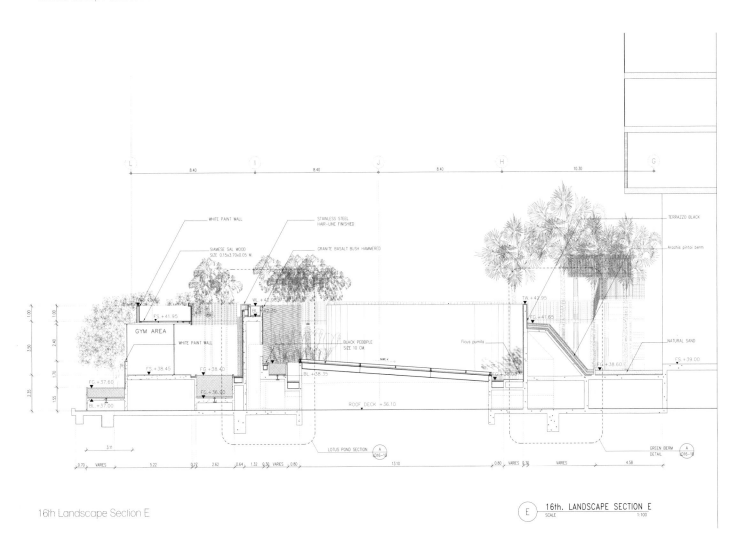

8.40   8.40   8.40   10.30

WHITE PAINT WALL

STAINLESS STEEL
HAIR-LINE FINISHIED

TERRAZZO BLACK

SIAMESE SAL WOOD
SIZE 0.15x3.70x0.05 M.

GRANITE BASALT BUSH HAMMERED

Arachis pintoi berm

TW. +42.95

WL. +42.95

BL. +38.20

TW. +42.95

FS. +41.95

1.00

1.00

GYM AREA

FS. +41.95

FS. +41.65

2.40

WHITE PAINT WALL

BLACK PEBBLE
SIZE 10 CM.

Ficus pumila

NATURAL SAND

3.50

1.70

FS. +38.45   FG +38.40   BL. +38.35   FS. +38.60   FS +39.00

FG +37.60   FG. +36.10

2.35

1.55

BL. +37.00

ROOF DECK +36.10

3.11

0.70   VARES   5.22   0.27   2.62   0.64   1.32 0.30 VARES   0.80   13.10   0.80 VARES 0.30   VARES   4.58

LOTUS POND SECTION
A
1016-18

GREEN BERM
DETAIL
A
1016-18

16th Landscape Section E

E   16th. LANDSCAPE SECTION E
SCALE   1:100

The Garden of Hilton Pattaya is basically built on a roof of a huge shopping mall, Central Festival Pattaya Beach.

When we got the commission to do the project, the mall was already built. So the structure can't be revised to make it the better site condition. When we first visit the site, we noticed three important elements:

1) There is a gigantic skylight in the middle of the roof. The Skylight is to bring Sunlight down to the mall, but it can't bear any load on it. So we can't use it as part of the Garden. What makes it worse is that Central didn't have Budget to decorate this Skylight at all, so it is half glass and half concrete, which we ended up putting faked grass on it.

2) Because the Skylight is right in the middle of the Roof, we ended up having only small and narrow areas around it for the Garden. Within our already-limited areas, we must locate Gym and Toilets somewhere as well.

3) The Mall has an interesting in and out facade. However, the irregular edge made it hard to design the clean and simple garden we want.

17th Floor Plan

Our first move is to deal with the area around the Skylight. We used the Resort Design Principle to divide and organize the roof into 3 Main Garden Parts.

1) Arrival Court. The hotel lobby is located on the 17th Floor. Once the guests get out of the elevators, this Arrival Court will be the first thing they see. We don't want the guests to see another guests walking around in Bikinis here, so we closed this area. The Concept of DEPT's Lobby Design is "Shallow Water", so we continued the story and cover our Arrival Court with sand and green landform.

2) Sun Deck. As mentioned above, we don't have much space left around the Skylight. However, a gym and toilets must be put in this already-tight space. So we proposed the idea of adding another Layer of Garden on top, by extending the gym and toilet Roof all the way to the Hotel. What we got is the Reasonable-size Deck with a direct access from 18th Floor (1 floor above the Lobby). The good thing is that guests who dress casually to swim, don't have to walk through the Lobby, which will be full of arriving and leaving Guests.

3) Ocean Pool. We don't have much choice about where to locate the Pool. This is the only area big enough to do so. However, there is a problem of the irregular edge of the mall. We try to avoid adding another complicate design here, so we just use one simple curve to define the Pool. Underneath the water, we separate the pool into Lap Pool, Fun Pool, Jacuzzi Maze, and Kid Pool. Inspired by Shiny School of Fish, we asked Dazzles, lighting designer, to add Fiber Optic on the bottom of the pool. So, at night, the Pool grows like those fish or stars...

TIPS

Air pool
Air pool settings have been very common in real estate development. Among them, Singapore Marina Bay Sands Hotel's air pool in the roof garden is renowned in the world.

Farmerson

COMMENT

The designer solves troubles on this harsh site without any hesitancy to create a relaxed and beautiful garden. It's a clever strategy to create a place for man to get closed to nature by artificial means.

"Where technology meets tranquility."

Rooftop Workplace of Tomorrow

Landscape Architect: Patricia Fox MSGD / MBALI
Location: RHS Chelsea Flower Show, London 2012
Site Area: 200 m^2
Photography: Benjamin Wetherall

CLIMATIC CONDITIONS

London belongs to temperate marine climate, warm in winter and cool in summer with small temperature difference. It rains throughout the year, especially in winters.

PLANTS

maple, himalayan birch, norway maple, buxus, thymus, yarrow, rocket candytuft, white campion

EDITOR'S CHOICE

This garden design challenged the perception of traditional work space, bringing innovate breakthrough for outdoor area design. The outdoor furniture' simple, technologic, fashionable corresponded with the planed well stratified plants, bring out a chic, create and office environment for white - collars.

Rooftop Workplace of Tomorrow is an extension of the working office which uses vacant urban rooftop space. The garden offers an innovative, thought-provoking environment that can be used by both individuals and groups. Individuals can sit in contemporary hanging chairs and network using a smart phone or tablet. Conferences can be held within the lounge area under the weatherproof canopy. This area has a 3m x 3m video/projection screen that projects sound and visuals, and is surrounded by beautiful planting (including a pick your own herbal tea bar). This garden challenges our perception of workplaces, and offers inspirational ideas for the future.

Rendering 1

Rendering 2

Rendering 3

The main focal plant will be a stunning Pleached Field Maple (Acer Campestre) to give some stature to the garden. A West Himalayan Birch (Betula Jaquemontii) will provide subtle shade under which to relax on the chic bench, and the ashy bark will be complimented by the white flora throughout the garden. A Norway Maple (Acer Globosum) has been selected to provide a natural 'umbrella' for the floating workstation. Buxus cubes, Thymus balls and buxus hedging will provide the necessary structure to the garden, mimicking the 'rounded square' iPad inspired shape which is used consistently throughout the garden.

Furniture in the garden will be manufactured using brand new 'up-cycled' materials launched this year by Thomas Bramwell including their modern take on the egg chair and quirky hanging 'C' shaped chairs hung from a modern white metal pergola, as well as ultra chic bespoke 'star' sofa and chairs.

TIPS

Outdoor Office
With the technology development of portable office equipment, outdoor office is increasingly accepted. While outdoor office design comes to be appreciated by the public.

Calm and understated planting will be very textural, structured yet beautifully delicate. The planting scheme is a mix of green and silver blue foliage, and simple white flowering plants such as Yarrow (Achillea Millefolioum), Rocket Candytuft (Iberis Amara) and White Campion (Silene Latiflora).

Farmerson

COMMENT

The project has well illustrated the idea of "forms follows functions". The designer captures the new functional trend cleverly as a starting point and takes advantages of the site to present an extraordinary landscape space. As a result, everything in the garden seems terrific and natural.

"The enclosed clear and comfort."

Morningstar

Landscape Architect: Hoerr Schaudt Landscape Architects
Location: Chicago, USA

CLIMATIC CONDITIONS

Chicago is also known as the "Windy City". It belongs to temperate continental climate with distinct seasons. Subjected to the influence of Lake Michigan, it has great temperature different between winter and summer with sufficient rainfall.

PLANTS

euonymus coloratus, bulbs

EDITOR'S CHOICE

For the relatively small size of terrace space, the designer takes the simple planting way to create a spacious outdoor space with multipurpose uses, where staff can have meeting, private coffee break or group gathering.

The views from this roof showcase historic Chicago architecture, including the Reliance Building and the former Marshall Fields building. The surrounding buildings reach higher than the roof, and so the architecture creates a sense of enclosure. Because of this, and the relatively small size of the terrace, the design intent aimed to create a feeling of spaciousness.

Rooftop conditions are very harsh environments for plant material, so we must choose plants carefully and we thoroughly consider where the plantings will be placed on the roof. At Morningstar, we grouped everything closely together in a concentrated mass. Although there is more paving than vegetation on the roof, it does not look that way.

The client wanted the space to have multiple uses – employee meetings, private coffee-break conversations, and corporate parties—and this design was the most effective way to accomplish that. The benches within the plants allow for people to sit and talk to one another, and the seating on the paved area can be easily moved.

The plantings beneath the trees are simple and are concentrated together to achieve the appropriate scale for the space. The ground plane is planted with euonymus coloratus, a hardy goundcover that turns red in the fall and is able to withstand any reflective light that come off the building. Bulbs, like the aliums in the photo above, and rotations of annuals mark changes in the seasons.

TIPS

Euonymus fortunei 'Coloratus' (wintercreeper euonymus)
Growing in Shaanxi, Shanxi, Henan province and south of the Yangtze river.Yangtze River and turning to red in autumn. 'Colora (commonly called purple wintercreeper euonymus) is primarily a trailing ground cover form and spreads indefinitely by decorating the wall, stone, trees.

Farmerson

COMMENT

The design directly meets the functions required as a simple and accurate landscape space i.e. the open spaces enclosed by glass railings and paved areas for rest and meeting. In addition, the selected plants add visual richness to the space by their simplicity and elegance.

"Bustling Around, Display The Classical Flows."

The Museum of Modern Art Roof Garden

Landscape Architect: Ken Smith Landscape Architect
Client: The Museum of Modern Art
Location: New York, USA
Photography: Peter Mauss/ESTO

CLIMATIC CONDITIONS

New York is in temperate continental climate, warm in summer and cool in winter with obvious temperature difference. It has concentrate rainfalls and four distinct seasons.

PLANTS

boxwood

EDITOR'S CHOICE

The roof garden is composed of natural, recycled, synthetic materials, including natural stone, recycled glass and recycled rubber cover, fiberglass grating, PVC pipe, artificial boxwood plants, foam head and synthetic materials contains artificial rocks. Designers have conducted extensive research on manufacturing technology with these new materials to create the "American-style zen garden" straightly and narrowly.

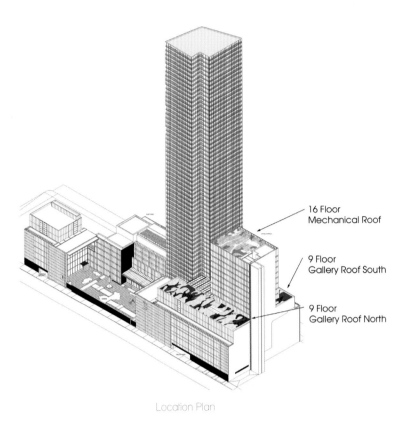

16 Floor
Mechanical Roof

9 Floor
Gallery Roof South

9 Floor
Gallery Roof North

Location Plan

The design draws inspiration from Japanese dry Zen gardens with a relatively flat garden of white gravel, recycled black rubber, crushed glass, sculptural stones and artificial boxwood plants. While rooted in tradition, the design and fabrication is contemporary in spirit and form.

The design started out most literally as a Xerox copy taken from a pair of skateboarder's camouflage pants. The pattern was scaled and fitted onto the roof area. The design was translated through the rigor of a reductive geometry of straight line segments, three distinct curve radii, and two intersection conditions. Extensive research was done on materials, material systems and fabrication techniques.

The MoMA roof garden material palette consists of natural, recycled and synthetic materials including natural crushed stone, recycled glass, recycled rubber mulch, as well as synthetic materials including fiberglass grating, PVC fittings, artificial boxwood plants, foam headers and artificial rocks. Contemporary C-N-C (computer-numerical-cutting) fabrication techniques were used to reduce on-site labor. All of the fiberglass panels and foam headers were factory-cut, using the landscape architect's CAD files as templates.

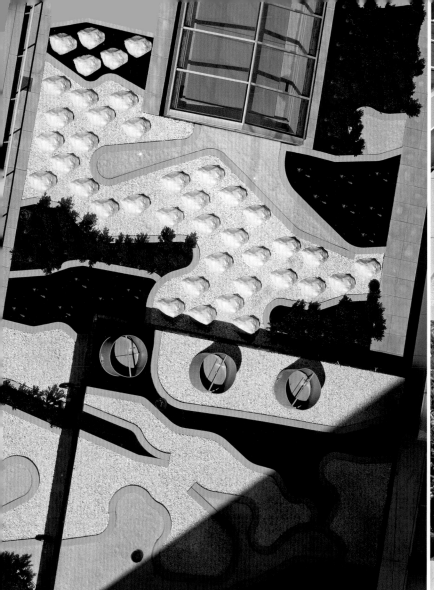

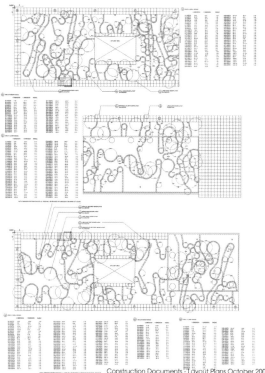

Construction Documents - Layout Plans October 2004

Layout Plan

Construction Documents - Materials Plan, October 2004

Material Plan

**9 Floor Gallery Roof
North and South:**

- Shrub Assembly
  Artificial Boxwood Shrubs
  Green Fiberglass Grating
  PVC Pipeds and Flanges

- Headers
  Polyurethane Coated Milled Foam

- Integral Color Boulders
  Black Synthetic Boulder
  White Synthetic Boulder

- Ground Covers
  Crushed Recycled Glass
  Recycled Black Rubber
  Crushed White Marble Chips

TIPS

Dry Landscape
It's a kind of Japanese garden creating a miniature stylized
landscape through carefully composed arrangements
of rocks, water features, moss, pruned trees and bushes
Gravel or sand are used to represent ripples in water.
and rocks for mountains. Dry landscape means "a dry
scenery" or "dry water and mountains", which was created
at temples of Zen Buddhism in Kyoto, Japan during the
Muromachi Period, Momoyama Period and Edo Period."

Farmerson

COMMENT

Modern "Dry Landscape" has appeared in the most suitable site as
the project shows us. "Dry Landscape" on the dry roof, such idea
has been presented by many designers, but few of them have combined modern art spirits, eco conception, advanced art design and
traditional dry landscape as the project does.

"A small platform embraces a big city."

Sydney City Rooftop Garden

Landscape Architect: Secret Gardens of Sydney
Location: Sydney, Australia
Photography: Jason Busch

CLIMATIC CONDITIONS

Sydney is in humid subtropical climate, hot and wet in summer, cool and dry in winter.

PLANTS

Buxus microphylla, Dietes robinsoniana, Raphiolepsis indica 'Snow maiden', Lavandula stoechas 'Avon View', Juniperus chinesis, Trachelospermum asiaticum, Gardenia augustifolia 'florida'

EDITOR'S CHOICE

Large wooden platform shows its feature through the gray paving. It forms an intense colorful contrast as a the transition zone to integrate the entire garden with surrounding buildings. The Attic seems to put on new clothes with the rooftop greenery. The roof garden provides private space with low-maintenance and high-enjoyment for People, and it is also a good party place.

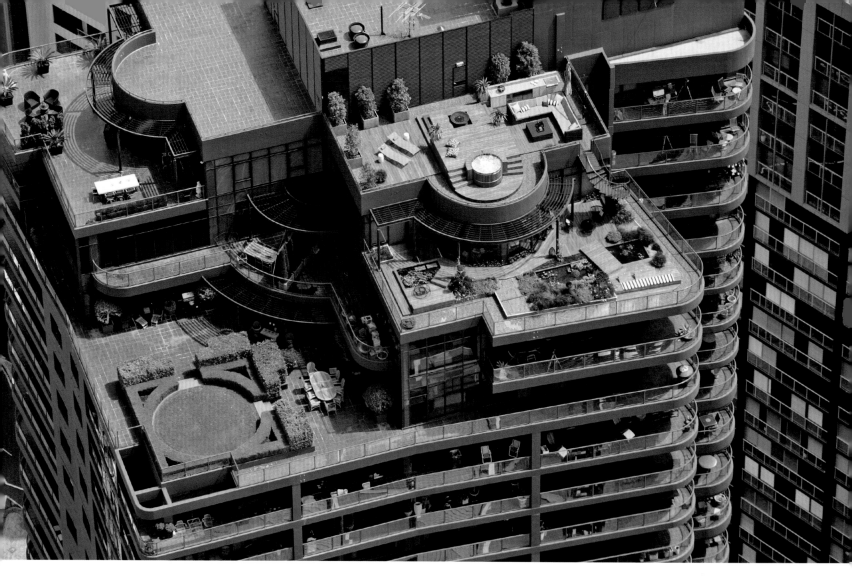

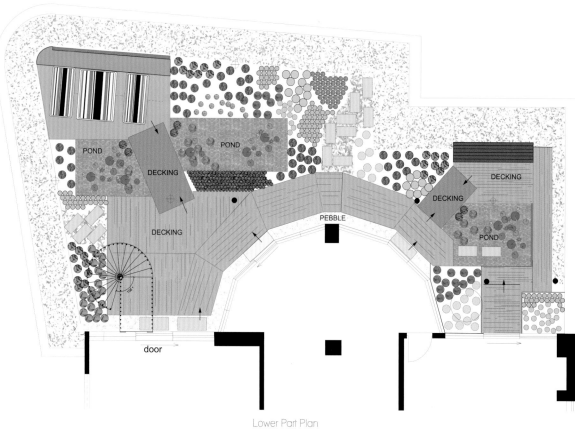

Lower Part Plan

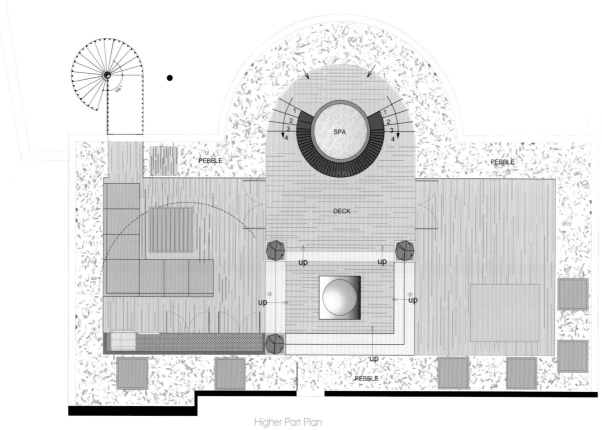

Higher Part Plan

This apartment is actually the floor below the penthouse that Secret Gardens had completed the year prior. With stringent building codes on what we could and could not do, we worked with the building management to ensure that the design and construction could meet the client's brief.

The result is a beautiful garden located 25 floors in the sky! Clean lines and a simple design, have created a spot to place a chair, sit in the middle of the city and enjoy the view. The low levels of hedging ensure the clients can now see the amazing view of Sydney harbour and the Opera House.

The design focused on renovating an existing garden that was currently obstructing the views from this city apartment. The style had to be consistent with the architecture of the building and the client's preference was a garden that was more formal in its approach. This was created with clean lines of Buxus hedging and topiary cones. The introduction of Iris and Lavender, soften the formal aspects and create a whimsical effect. The existing tiles on the balconies, and none of the external architecture of the building could be modified so all materials and plants selected need to be complimentary to these materials.

TIPS

Drip Irrigation System
Drip irrigation system specializes in extremely efficient irrigation technology, it is an irrigation facilities composed of water projects, central hub, water distribution network, drip equipment etc.

Plants used included: Buxus microphylla - Japanese Box; Dietes robinsoniana - Wedding Lilly; Raphiolepsis indica 'Snow maiden' - Indian Hawthorne; Lavandula stoechas 'Avon View' - Italian Lavender; Juniperus chinesis - Spartan Juniper; Trachelospermum asiaticum - Star Jasmine; Gardenia augustifolia 'florida' – Gardenia. The turf is artificial so therefore does not require water. The plant beds were less than 300mm so drainage cell was used in the planters to create a cavity for waterflow. The garden beds are run on a drop irrigation system. The garden has now been in place for about 3 years and is thriving with very little maintenance. We maintain the garden every 8 weeks.

Song Sheng

COMMENT

The rooftop garden design cares for functional and aesthetic values, which carries out its conception and functions onto the entire spaces. Functions of leisure and gathering are strengthened here. Leaning on the transparent glass railings, people can appreciate the skyline, panoramic views of the city and artificial landscape around. Local plants are chosen for local climate, such as lavender, gardenia, which adds fragrance to the garden. This enclosed space is friendly and intimate divided into different areas by clear pools and trails, where offers a chance for residents to re-know each other and develop a further relationship. Taking into account the working environment on the roof, drip irrigation system is applied to reduce energy consumption for sustainability.

"Show simple fashion in deep prosperity"

Rooftop Garden Inner City

Landscape Architect: Secret Gardens of Sydney
Location: Sydney, Australia
Photography: Jason Busch

CLIMATIC CONDITIONS

Sydney is in humid subtropical climate, hot and wet in summer, cool and dry in winter.

PLANTS

Buxus, shrub, iris, lavender

EDITOR'S CHOICE

A big lawn makes the small space seemed big. Boxwood hedge, conical shrub, irises, lavender and lotus pond close to the sink wood floor and brick, form a layered effect. Leisure wooden chair invites people to enjoy the port scenery.

Hidden over 25 floors above the city this green sculptured rooftop garden sits in the middle of skyscrapers. It is designed by Secret Gardens, creating a leisure place for the residents to leave far from the madding crowd and the noise.

Landscape design focuses on expanding the scope of vision, and at the same time create a visual effect like oases. On the landscape configuration, overall Garden is a circular, spread from a center to both sides, a green lawn open the vision, white chairs in the middle to the lawn make the landscape seems different, easy and comfort. While the centre is covered by Buxus hedging and topiary cones, and it is become another light point. External wooden furniture added a tranquil and comfortable atmosphere for the entire garden. People can overlook the enchanting panoramic view of Sydney from the garden.

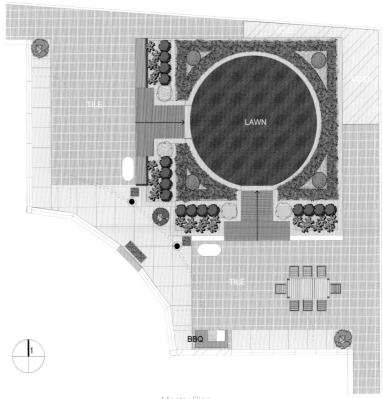

Master Plan

TIPS

IRIS
Iris was IRIS plants, it is an umbrella name of herbaceous
flowering plant. The flower consist of 6 petal-shaped leaves
coated, 3 or 6 stamens and the ovary coverd by flower pedicel.
it is located in Japan, China, Siberia, Central France, and
almost the whole temperate zone. It is the France national flower.

Song Sheng

COMMENT

In this small garden, the designer creates an open green landscape by minimalist design techniques, thus a pure and green balcony for the residents is born with open panoramic views. The wooden furniture adds a quiet and pleasing atmosphere for the garden. Rich greenery offers a comfortable and casual environment for visitors and also improves microclimate in the garden. The boxwood and manicured plants are highlight in the garden.

"Low - key Luxury hidden beside Huangpu River."

The Waterhouse at South Bund

Landscape Architect: Neri & Hu Design and Research Office
Client: Cameron Holdings Hotel Management Limited
Location: Shanghai, China
Site Area: 800 m²
Photography: Derryck Menere

CLIMATIC CONDITIONS

Shanghai belongs to the subtropical monsoon climate, the annual average temperature is 22.4 ℃ , annual rainfall is more than 2,100 mm. From July to September are the rainy seasons, the amount of precipitation occupies two-fifths in a year.

EDITOR'S CHOICE

The combination of humble cement tree pool and vegetation shows a unique rustic charm. Simple outdoor furniture in different tones tells a dialogue between old and new, corresponding to the renovation of boutique hotel, enhancing a human feel and giving the old architecture a new appearance.

Roof Plan

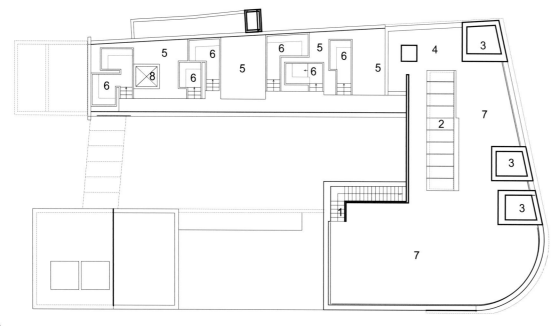

0 0.5 1   5 m

1 stair to roof bar
2 skylight
3 periscope
4 bar
5 sunken garden
6 seating pocket
7 seating area
8 void to guest room

Located by the new Cool Docks development on the South Bund District of Shanghai, the Waterhouse is a four-story, 19-room boutique hotel. And the project is located on the top of the fourth layer. The boutique hotel fronts the Huangpu River and looks across at the gleaming Pudong skyline. The architectural concept behind NHDRO's renovation rests on a clear contrast of what is old and new. Neri & Hu's structural addition, on the fourth floor, resonates with the industrial nature of the ships which pass through the river, providing an analogous contextual link to both history and local culture.

Strip flooring style eliminate the heavy and monotony that brought by reinforced concrete, and collocation with old walls, reflects old Shanghai customs, visually integrated into the inherit culture. Highlight of project is the riverside location, standing in the garden, embracing the beautiful scenery of Huangpu River. While

all kinds of plants in the garden, replacing a once desolate space with a kind of tranquil green grotto and contemplative place to pause.

The project is expressed through both a blurring and inversion of the interior and exterior, as well as between the public and private realms, creating a disorienting yet refreshing spatial experience for the hotel guest who longs for an unique five-star hospitality experience. The public spaces allow one to peek into private rooms while the private spaces invite one to look out at the public arenas, such as the large vertical room window above the reception desk and the corridor windows overlooking the dining room. These visual connections of unexpected spaces not only bring an element of surprise, but also force the hotel guests to confront the local Shanghai urban condition where visual corridors and adjacencies in tight nong-tang's define the unique spatial flavor of the city.

TIPS

Boutique hotel
Boutique hotel often contains luxury facilities in varying sizes in unique or intimate settings with full service accommodations. Sometimes known as "design hotels" or "lifestyle hotels", boutique hotels began appearing in the 1980s in major cities like London, New York, and San Francisco. Typically boutique hotels are furnished in a themed, stylish and/or aspirational manner.

Lyndon Neri, Rossana Hu

COMMENT

The original concrete building has been restored while new additions built over the existing structure were made using Cor-Ten steel, reflecting the industrial past of this working dock by the Huangpu River.

"Zen tells a different amorous style."

Zense Gourmet Deck and Lounge Panorama

Landscape Architect: T.R.O.P terrains + open space
Client: Central Retails Corp., Zen Department Store
Location: Bangkok, Thailand
Site Area: 900 m²
Cost: $ 300,000

CLIMATIC CONDITIONS

Bangkok belongs to the typical tropical monsoon climate. Influenced by Asian southwest monsoon and northeast monsoon, it has high temperature all the year round, the climate here stays stable with ample rainfall.

EDITOR'S CHOICE

The 4 elements: Earth, Water, Wind, and Fire are blended into design to creat a zen world on the 17th floor, Where one can enjoy the central cityscape of Bangkok. A quiet Zen Landscape is created though the designer just adopts simple materials and local cheap vegetation. It has greatly improved the ecological value of this project.

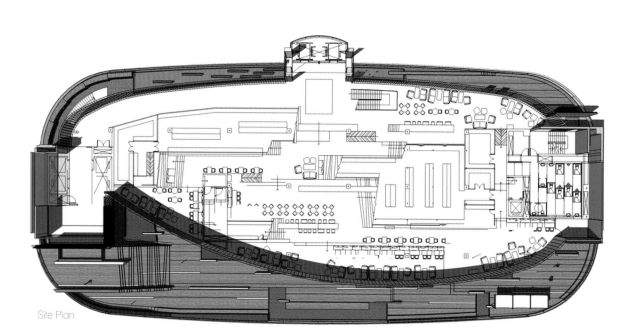

Site Plan

Zense Gourmet Deck is the first of the 4 new destinations, created by Zen World of Central Retails Corp. The main concept is the 4 elements, Earth, Water, Wind, and Fire. Zense's design inspiration comes from the Earth theme. The location of the project is on the roof top of Zen World, which is on the 17th floor. Here, we have one of the best views of Bangkok's central area.

The main feature of this place is the unobstructed panoramic view. So our first design move is to make sure that we could even make the view nicer.

TROP's goal is to create interesting space, using just one material, and also to make it Mute yet Urbane atmosphere. Also we want to create special aexperience for anyone who has a chance to visit the restaurant.

The total exterior area is about 900 sqm approx. The problem is that client wanted to add as many seats as possible. Also one major concern is that the existing shape of the deck is not rectangular, but rather half oval shape. So we started by creating interesting seating arrangements for each zone of the deck. In the end, we create some level differences in our main deck, in order to divide the space into several zones, main dining area, private zone, and sky bar.

As agree from the beginning, the main material of the place must be Wood, to represent the earth theme. We select the local wood plank, which is easy to find and can stand the extreme temperature of Bangkok's summer. The key is to pick a thicker piece, so it will not bend.

Unlike most high end restaurants, which normally use the most expensive plants available, the plantings for Zense Gourmet Deck are basically the unwanted species.

We use local plants, which normally grow at street sides, vacant lots, or dirty canals in Bangkok, in order to recreate the sense of place in this restaurant.

However, we design, arrange and compose those plantings in a more modern way. The result is quite interesting. People always know these plants, but never appreciate the beauty of them. They thought the plants are cheap and dirty. After they saw our design, they have changed their perception of the plants. They start to see them beautiful and cool looking once again.

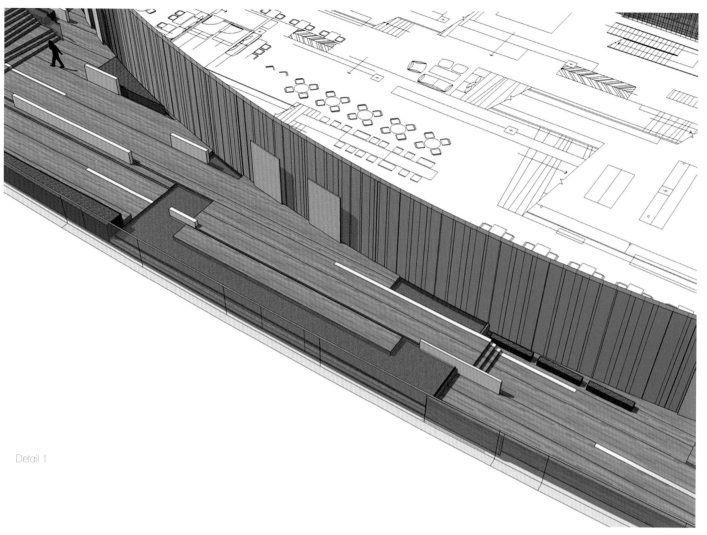

Detail 1

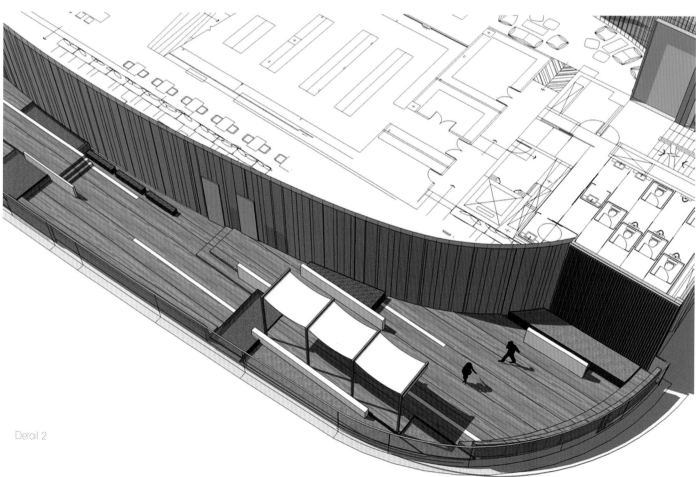

Detail 2

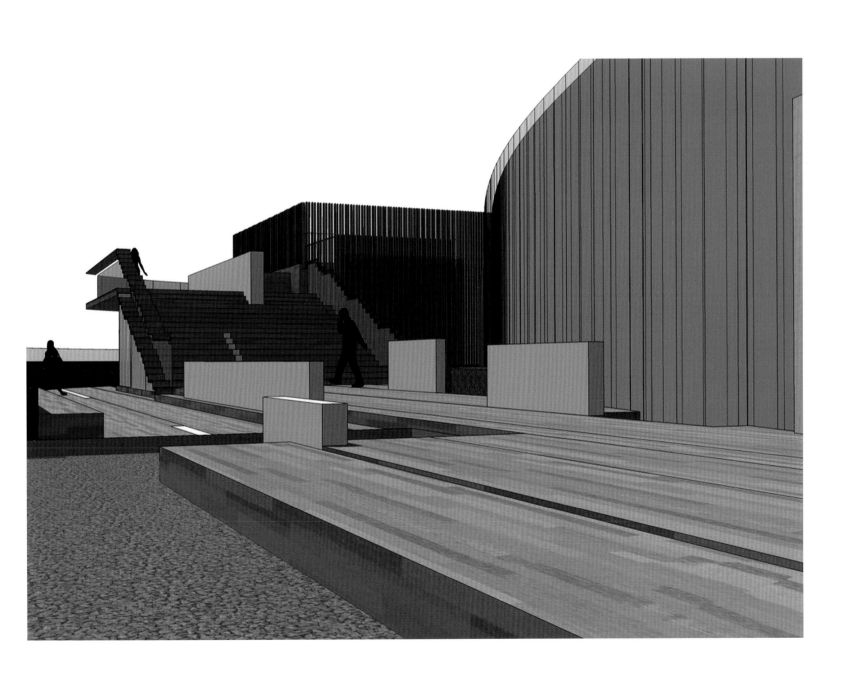

TIPS

Zen design
Design due to infiltration of Zen philosophy, modern art design shows unique silent and spiritual atmosphere. Zen design has always demonstrated a outside natural empty,giving a quiet and ethereal mood beyond imagination. Artists only make combination of spirits and physical, to feel the lonely Zen.

COMMENT

The use of refined design language and flexibility makes the project shined brightly. Located in this area with appropriate climates, the rooftop garden featured in independent and open will become a nice outdoor activity place for people.

Farmerson

"Even if you are in a concrete jungle, you will find a different world when you look up."

Citywalk 1 & Citywalk 2

Jointly developed by the Urban Renewal Authority, Sino Group
Location: Hong Kong, China
Image courtesy of Urban Renewal Authority

CLIMATIC CONDITIONS

Hong Kong belongs to subtropical region, with hot and humid summer as well as cool and dry winter. It rains frequently from May to September. Typhoons sometimes come between summer and autumn.

PLANTS

Ferns

EDITOR'S CHOICE

Citywalk is the first and largest green shopping mall in Hong Kong. It features a green space of over 743 m². Stepping into the mall feels like being in a forest. Its Vertical Garden plays a key role in reducing ambient temperatures, providing thermal insulation, acoustical control and purifying air.

Citywalk is a joint venture between the Urban Renewal Authority and Sino Land Company Limited. It is the first and largest green shopping mall in Hong Kong featuring a green space of over 743 m². It also won the Gold Award at the inaugural Skyrise Greenery Awards 2012.

Stepping into Citywalk 1 & Citywalk 2 would make one feel like stepping into an oasis. The walls in the plazza are covered by carefully selected plants in an orderly and systematic manner. Ferns growing on the walls survive on high quality of air and moisture, adding vitality and greening to the plazza. They also act as an air quality purifier ambient environment. The greenery has been planted on the wall since 2006, making the development a pioneer in eco-friendly buildings.

Greenery in Citywalk has a significant impact on the development of environmentally-friendly buildings and proves to be sustainable. Highlight of the shopping mall is a Vertical Wall on which plants are grown and act as natural heat insulators to reduce ambient temperatures, provide thermal insulation, acoustical control and purify the air. With its 11 distinctive green features and designs, Citywalk has been rated Platinum by the HK-BEAM Society.

The Gold Award does not only recognise the greenery in the mall, but also the overall environmentally-friendly design of Citywalk. For example, the cross ventilation entrance of the mall allows breezes to blow into the open plazza in hot summer, while the open plazza is connected to nearby streets for the convenience of residents. Furthermore, the landscaped water features, green pavement and shade trees in the plazza make it a perfect place to enjoy the summer.

TIPS

Green wall

There are two main kinds of green walls: green façades and living walls. Green façades are made up of climbing plants either growing directly on a wall or, more recently, specially designed supporting structures. The plant shoot system grows up the side of the building while being rooted in the ground. With a living wall the modular panels often consist of stainless steel containers, geotextiles, irrigation systems, a growing medium and vegetation.

Farmerson

COMMENT

Landscape is the best medium for man and nature. People are thirsting for nature as they are in a dense artificial environment, where "nature" appeared being precious. However, creating "nature" in an artificial environment is difficult as well. The project introduces natural elements in horizontal and vertical layers to bring in vitality to the artificial environment with dense population, which allows the design to be a classic and popular one.

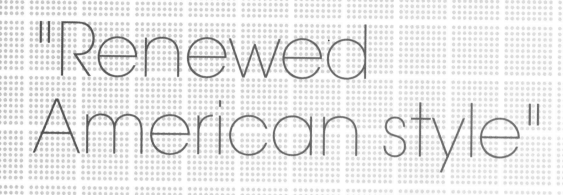

"Renewed American style"

Olympic Sculpture Park

Architecture & Site Design: WEISS/MANFREDI Architecture/Landscape/Urbanism
Client: Seattle Art Museum
Location: Seattle, Washington, USA
Site Area: Park: 36,421 m² Pavilion: 1,672.25 m²
Photography: Benjamin Benschneider, Paul Warchol, WEISS/MANFREDI Architecture/
Landscape/Urbanism

CLIMATIC CONDITIONS

Seattle is in temperate marine climate, warm in winter and cool in summer with a small temperature difference troughout the year. It rains throughout the year, especially in winter.

PLANTS

fir, cedar, hemlock, ginkgo, Dawn redwood, perennials, ferns, pines

EDITOR'S CHOICE

Winner of an international design competition, the design for the Olympic Sculpture Park capitalizes on the forty-foot grade change from the top of the site to the water's edge. Planned as a continuous landscape that wanders from the city to the shoreline, this Z-shaped hybrid landform provides a new pedestrian infrastructure.As the route descends from the pavilion to the water, it links three distinct settings: a dense and temperate evergreen forest; a deciduous forest of seasonally changing characteristics; and a shoreline garden including a series of new tidal terraces for salmon habitat and saltwater vegetation.

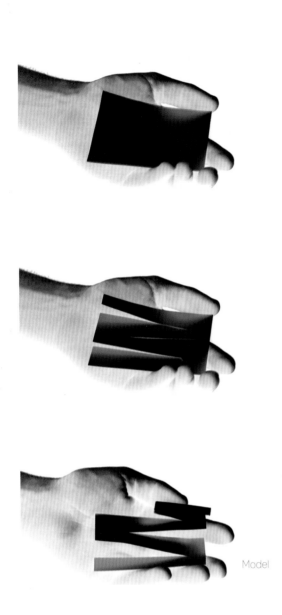

Model

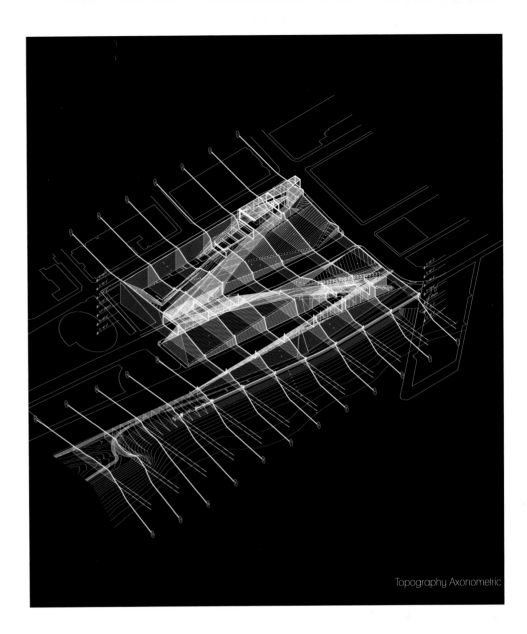

Topography Axonometric

Envisioned as a new urban model for sculpture parks, this project is located on Seattle's last undeveloped waterfront property – an industrial brownfield site sliced by train tracks and an arterial road. The design connects three separate sites with an uninterrupted Z-shaped "green" platform, descending forty feet from the city to the water, capitalizing on views of the skyline and Elliott Bay, and rising over existing infrastructure to reconnect the urban core to the revitalized waterfront.

TIPS

Sloping Rooftop Garden
With the development of parametric design, landscape is more and more combined with topography, architecture, structure and make the whole project integrate part. Lots of outstanding projects come out in recent years that contributes to a deep integration of architecture and landscape by a slope rooftop garden design.

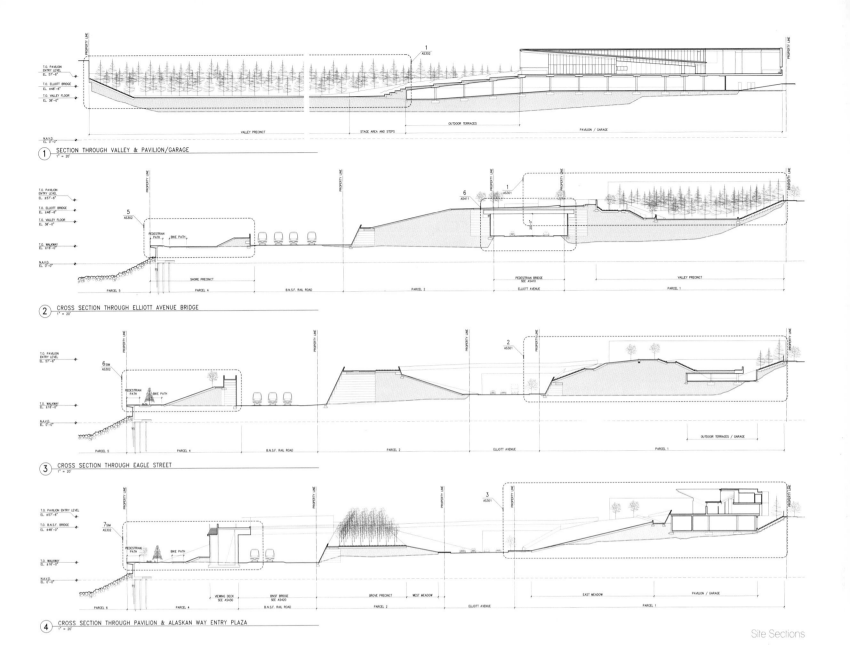

T.O. PAVILION
ENTRY
EL. 57'-6"

T.O. ELLIOTT BRIDGE
EL. ±48'-6"

T.O. VALLEY FLOOR
EL. 38'-0"

N.A.V.D.
EL. 0'-0"

| VALLEY PRECINCT | STAGE AREA AND STEPS | OUTDOOR TERRACES | PAVILION / GARAGE |

① SECTION THROUGH VALLEY & PAVILION/GARAGE
1" = 20'

T.O. PAVILION
ENTRY LEVEL
EL. ±57'-6"

T.O. ELLIOTT BRIDGE
EL. ±48'-6"

T.O. VALLEY FLOOR
EL. 38'-0"

T.O. WALKWAY
EL. ±18'-0"

N.A.V.D.
EL. 0'-0"

PEDESTRIAN PATH | BIKE PATH

| PARCEL 5 | PARCEL 4 | B.N.S.F. RAIL ROAD | PARCEL 2 | ELLIOTT AVENUE | PARCEL 1 |
| SHORE PRECINCT | | | | PEDESTRIAN BRIDGE SEE AS410 | VALLEY PRECINCT |

② CROSS SECTION THROUGH ELLIOTT AVENUE BRIDGE
1" = 20'

T.O. PAVILION
ENTRY LEVEL
EL. 57'-6"

T.O. WALKWAY
EL. ±18'-0"

N.A.V.D.
EL. 0'-0"

PEDESTRIAN PATH | BIKE PATH

| PARCEL 5 | PARCEL 4 | B.N.S.F. RAIL ROAD | PARCEL 2 | ELLIOTT AVENUE | PARCEL 1 |
| | | | | | OUTDOOR TERRACES / GARAGE |

③ CROSS SECTION THROUGH EAGLE STREET
1" = 20'

T.O. PAVILION ENTRY LEVEL
EL. ±57'-6"

T.O. B.N.S.F. BRIDGE
EL. ±48'-0"

T.O. WALKWAY
EL. ±18'-0"

N.A.V.D.
EL. 0'-0"

PEDESTRIAN PATH | BIKE PATH

| PARCEL 6 | PARCEL 4 | B.N.S.F. RAIL ROAD | PARCEL 2 | ELLIOTT AVENUE | PARCEL 1 |
| | VIEWING DECK SEE AS430 | BNSF BRIDGE SEE AS420 | GROVE PRECINCT | WEST MEADOW | EAST MEADOW | PAVILION / GARAGE |

④ CROSS SECTION THROUGH PAVILION & ALASKAN WAY ENTRY PLAZA
1" = 20'

Site Sections

Winner of an international design competition, the Olympic Sculpture Park capitalizes on the forty-foot grade change from the top of the site to the water's edge. Planned as a continuous landscape that wanders from the city to the shore line, this Z-shaped hybrid landform provides a new pedestrian infrastructure.

Built with a system of mechanically stabilized earth, the enhanced landform re-establishes the original topography of the site, as it crosses the highway and train tracks and descends to meet the city. Layered over the existing site and infrastructure, the scheme creates a dynamic link that makes the waterfront accessible.

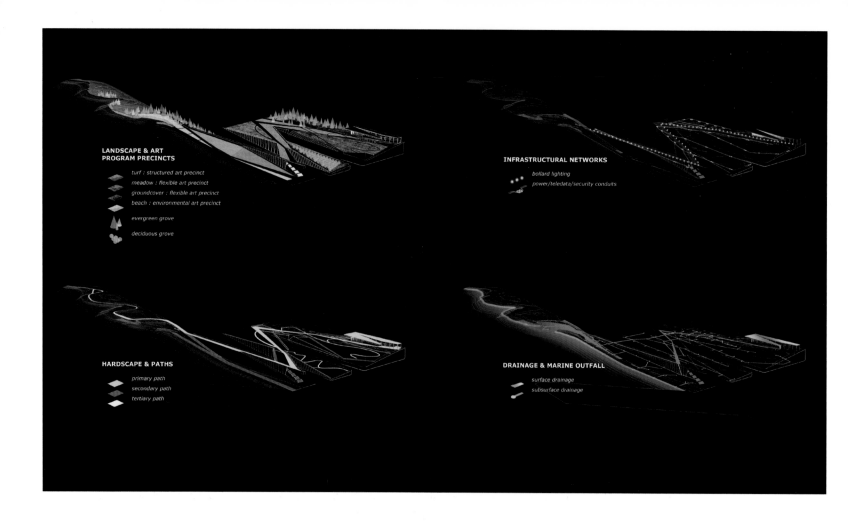

LANDSCAPE & ART PROGRAM PRECINCTS

- turf : structured art precinct
- meadow : flexible art precinct
- groundcover : flexible art precinct
- beach : environmental art precinct
- evergreen grove
- deciduous grove

INFRASTRUCTURAL NETWORKS

- bollard lighting
- power/teledata/security conduits

HARDSCAPE & PATHS

- primary path
- secondary path
- tertiary path

DRAINAGE & MARINE OUTFALL

- surface drainage
- subsurface drainage

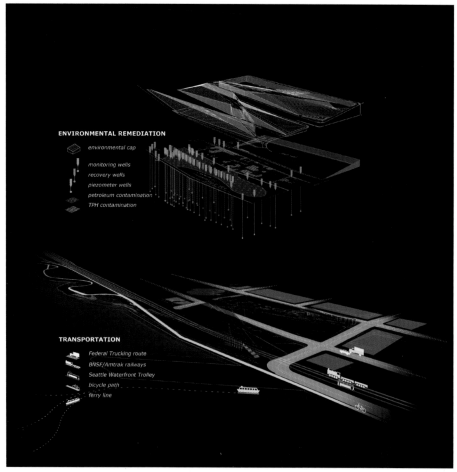

ENVIRONMENTAL REMEDIATION

- environmental cap
- monitoring wells
- recovery wells
- piezometer wells
- petroleum contamination
- TPH contamination

TRANSPORTATION

- Federal Trucking route
- BNSF/Amtrak railways
- Seattle Waterfront Trolley
- bicycle path
- ferry line

As a "landscape for art", the Olympic Sculpture Park defines a new experience for modern and contemporary art outside the museum walls. The topographically varied park provides diverse settings for sculpture of multiple scales. Deliberately open-ended, the design invites new interpretations of art and environmental engagement, reconnecting the fractured relationships of art, landscape, and urban life.

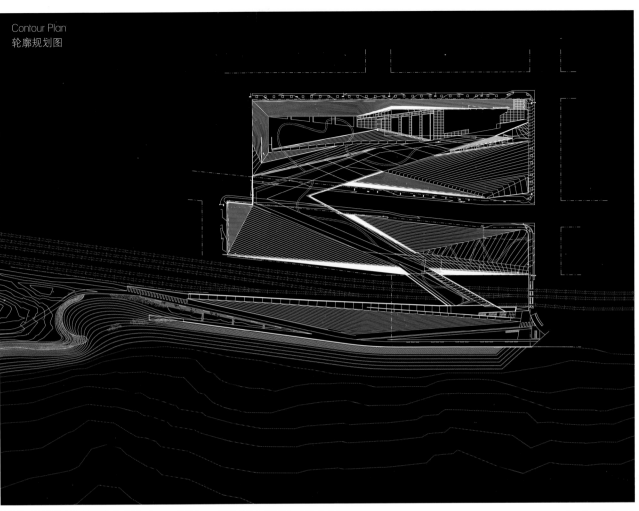

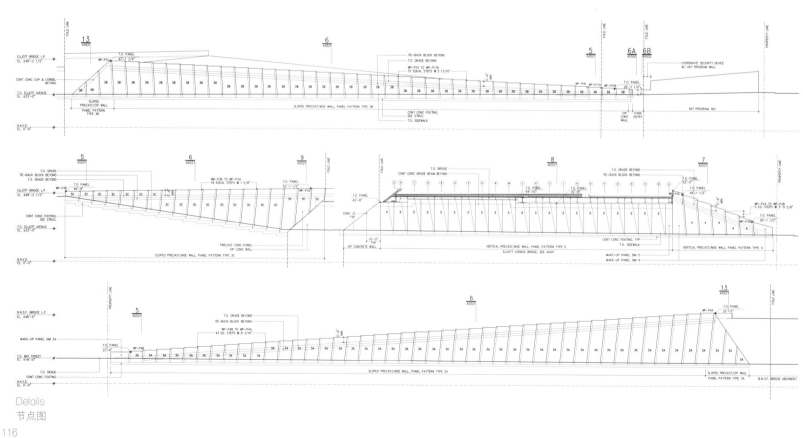

Details
节点图

The main pedestrian route is initiated at an 18,000-square-foot exhibition pavilion and descends as each leg of the path opens to radically different views. The first stretch crosses a highway, offering views of the Olympic Mountains; the second crosses the train tracks, offering views of the city and port; and the last descends to the water, offering views of the newly created beach. This pedestrian landform now allows free movement between the city's urban center and the restored beaches at the waterfront. As the route descends from the pavilion to the water, it links three distinct settings: a dense and temperate evergreen forest; a deciduous forest of seasonally changing characteristics; and a shoreline garden including a series of new tidal terraces for salmon habitat and saltwater vegetation.

Throughout the park, landforms and plantings collaborate to direct, collect, and cleanse storm water as it moves through the site before being discharged into Elliott Bay.

COMMENT

"Our fundamental aspiration was to create a sculpture park at the intersection of the city and Puget Sound, defining a new model for bringing art to the public and the public to the park. Our intent was to establish connections where separations existed, inventing a setting that brings art, city, and Sound together – implicitly questioning where the art begins and where it ends."

Marion Weiss, Michael Manfredi

"Aroma, rhyme, fragrance, sprinkle in mind."

Rooftop Garden of Ewha Women's University

Landscape Architect: Dominique Perrault Architecture
Client: Ewha Campus Center Project T/F, Ewha Women's University
Location: Seoul, South Korea
Site Area: 31,000 m²
Photography: Gaëlle Lauriot-Prévost, Dominique Perrault, André Morin, Luca Reale, Frederico de Matteis, Suk Joon YOON, Ewha Women's University

CLIMATIC CONDITIONS

Seoul has a temperate monsoon climate. The annual average temperature is 11.8 °C, with four distinct seasons. Springs and autumns rain a little in a warm climate; summers keep on continuous heat and rainy weathers; temperature in winters slightly lower than other cities of the same latitude.

PLANTS

pear tree

EDITOR'S CHOICE

Design concept of the underground university creates a large green area for the campus. The elements of underground architecture, green landscape, and landscape fault contribute to this slope-roof garden. The green roof and ground level are linked closely to offer an outdoor space for students. In addition to the aesthetic breakthrough, the roof garden also brings many ecological benefits for the surroundings.

The new campus centre of the University of Ewha will accomodates 20,000 students. It includes spaces for study and sport, offices, a cinema and car parks.

A landscape then, more than an architecture work, located in the midst of Seoul's university area. A campus valley where nature, sport grounds, event locations and educational buildings mix, intermingle and follow one another. A long asphalted strip, delineated at one end by a race track, and completely surrounded by nature. Arranged nature where pear trees and topiary reign. Black asphalt, red race track, green nature and finally the white brightness of the valley appears. A valley, which is bravely drawn in the ground, slides down along a gentle slope. At the other end of the valley, the slope becomes a huge stairway which can be used as an open air amphitheatre if necessary.

The idea of this underground university was born out of the desire to preserve a large green space in the centre of the university campus. The six-storey building is organized around a long ramp sloping down in opposition with the gently rising natural topography. The two large glass curtain walls facing the external circulation ramp serve as elements for day lighting and allow for natural ventilation of parts of the building as well.

The specificity of this building is the link between the architectural concepts and the sustainable strategies adopted. In fact, the first architectural ideas (underground building, green garden, landscape fracture) that give its strong identity to the building enable extraordinary performances in terms of sustainability.

Besides the aesthetic and psychological benefits, numerous ecological benefits include the recovery of green space in this area of Seoul, moderation of the urban heat island effect, improved storm-water management, water and air purification and a reduction in energy consumption. Specific benefits include:

Enhanced Ecology - The roof offers dramatic biodiversity benefits including the provision of valuable habitats for nationally important species. The roof will absorb particulate pollution and airborne pollutants and contributes to noise reduction.

Mitigation of storm water - The rapid run-off from roof surfaces can often result in flooding or extensive increase in drainage capacity. A major benefit of green roofs is their ability to absorb storm-water and release it slowly over a period of several hours.

Improved roof temperature - The protection of fluctuations in temperature helps reduce internal energy consumption. As a consequence, the classrooms under the green roof are more stable providing greater comfort to users.

Water efficiency - The benefits of the proposed green roof have been described. In addition to this, measures to reduce potable water consumption have been used including low water using fittings, Rainwater collection: rainwater is collected from the roof, stored, and then used as the needs arise.

TIPS

Sloping Rooftop Garden Design

To lay a natural green field on a slope roof, several problems must be done, such as water storage and drainage system, soil slipping in different layers, etc. Slop roof generally appropriate to drought-tolerant plants, shrubs and grass. The conservation is better to drip irrigation, auto-sprinkling or manual. One point should noticed that slope roof will have a faster drainage and a water-losing soil, early planted plants shall have frequent watering and maintenance.

COMMENT

The right combination of landscape and architecture makes the project a "thick green layer" covered on the building, where landscape on the ground continues growing on the roof. The unique handling blurs the edge between traditional and natural landscape, combining them as a boundaryless part. Conforming to the architectural form, the eco roof greenery helps to increase bio-diversity on the campus and also well solve the building's heat absorption and loss. The combination of landscape and architecture, greenery and site are telling that future landscape urbanism will be realized in more design industries.

Song Sheng

"The Way to Seek Happiness, Nothing but Live a Natural Life."

The Gary Comer Youth Center Roof Garden

Landscape Architect: Hoerr Schaudt Landscape Architects
Client: Gary Comer Youth Center
Location: Chicago, USA
Site Area: 758 m²

CLIMATIC CONDITIONS

Chicago is in temperate continental climate, warm in summer and cool in winter with obvious temperature difference. It has concentrate rainfalls in certain periods and four distinct seasons.

PLANTS

fruits, vegetables, herbs and flowers, cabbage, sunflowers, carrots, lettuce, strawberries

EDITOR'S CHOICE

This beautiful and restful place instead of a typical farm not only promotes gardening knowledge for adolescents, but also enhances their environmental awareness production. Fruit, vegetable, herb and flowers here turn it into a "happy farm" for children.

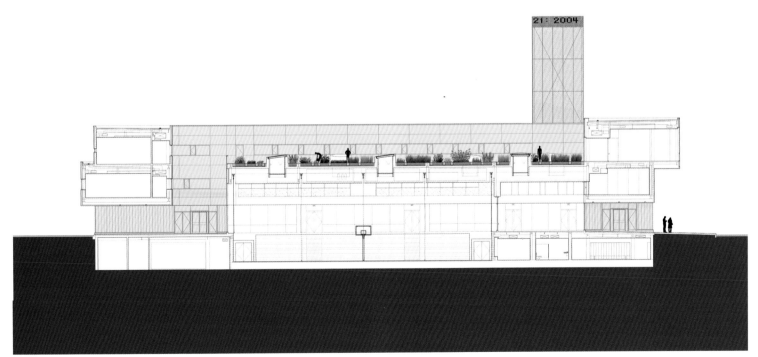

Section

The Gary Comer Youth Center Roof Garden is an after-school learning space for youth and seniors in a neighborhood with little access to safe outdoor environments. Last year alone, it produced over 1,000 pounds of organic food used by students, local restaurants and the center's café. Sleek and graphic, it turns the typical working vegetable garden into a place of beauty and respite.

Located in Chicago's Grand Crossing neighborhood, the Gary Comer Youth Center offers a safe, welcoming after-school space for indoor activity. Its 8,160-square-foot green roof is a model for using traditionally underutilized space for urban agriculture and exceptional in its balance of an aesthetic vision with practical needs.

The landscape architect worked closely with the architect and donor to develop a vision for a green roof to include a flower and working vegetable garden, and suggested that the center employ a full-time garden manager to enhance educational program development and manage maintenance. The result is a garden used in extremely creative ways for horticultural learning, environmental awareness, and food production.

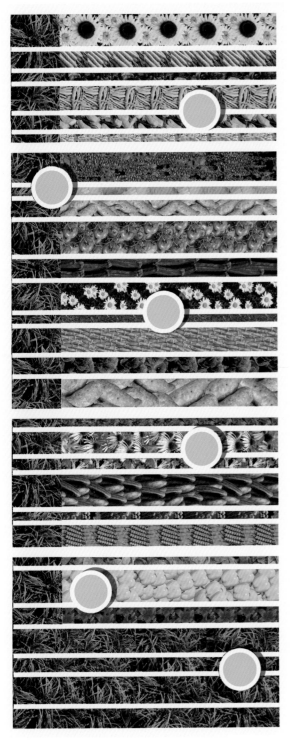

Sunflower Mixture
with Tulip Bulbs

Carrots

Purple Leaf Lettuce

Beans

Hot Peppters

Oregano / Basil

Foxglove Mixture
with Daffodil Bulbs

Cabbage

Sweet Potato

Tomato

Zucchini

Daisy / Aster Mixture
with Tulip Bulbs

Rosemary / Dill

Okra

Romaine Lettuce

Potato

Parsley

Coneflower / Beard Tongue Mixture
with Muscari Bulbs

Broccoli

Cucumber

Chives

Peas

Butterhead Lettuce

Yellow Bell Pepper

Lily Mixture
with Tulip Bulbs

Creeping Lilyturf

While reducing climate control costs and providing an outdoor classroom, the green roof is able to withstand enthusiastic children digging for potatoes and carrots with garden tools. Soils 18–24 inches deep allow for viable food production, including cabbage, sunflowers, carrots, lettuce and strawberries. Sharp differences between ground temperatures and those on the roof mean that the rooftop is in a different climate zone and can be utilized throughout the winter. The resulting garden, only three years old, is still evolving.

Located on the second floor over the center's gymnasium, the garden is surrounded by the circulation corridor and classrooms of the third floor. Floor-to-ceiling windows transform this working garden into a highly graphic viewing garden as students move from one classroom to another. Plastic lumber made from recycled milk containers forms pathways within the garden that align with the courtyard garden's window frames. Metal circles scattered throughout the garden serve as elements of artistic expression even as they function as skylights, bringing outdoor illumination to the building's gymnasium and café below.

TIPS

Rooftop Farming
Rooftop farming is the cultivation of food on the roof of a building. In many ways, rooftop farming is a specialized application of what is often referred to as a 'roof garden'. In addition to the aesthetic, recreational, ecological, and architectural benefits provided by roof gardens, rooftop farming focuses on local food production supplies for its maintainers and the community promotes small-scale local agriculture food resources.

Song Sheng

COMMENT

The rooftop garden is aim to provide a safe and popular extracurricular space for children through an innovative pattern design to well balance visual and practical needs. Vegetable planted on the roof helps to regulate indoor temperature, collect rainwater and reduce water pressure. It also forms an insulation layer, thereby reducing the use of air conditioning and cost caused by climate change. In the garden, children can enjoy pleasure of labor and fresh air, pick the fruits planted by themselves, or even get a windfall. It's a nice garden for people get close to nature, appreciate the environment.

"A flower, a world;
A grass, a heaven."

Roof Garden for Great Ormond Street Hospital for Children

Landscape Architect: Andy Sturgeon Landscape and Garden Design
Client: NHS Trust, Great Ormond Street Hospital for Children
Location: London, UK
Site Area: 261 m²

CLIMATIC CONDITIONS

London belongs to temperate marine climate, warm in winter and cool in summer with small temperature difference. It rains throughout the year, especially in winters.

EDITOR'S CHOICE

Through the layering created by the trees, statues, fences, vegetation, lawns, roads with lively colors, the project echoes the psychology, physiology and growth characteristics of children. Taking into account the usefulness for the hospital staff, semi-private space s are also being created. This is a bold attempt to improve the hospital environment.

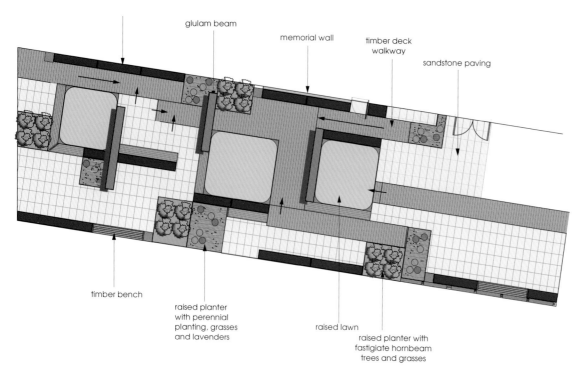

glulam beam

memorial wall

timber deck
walkway

sandstone paving

timber bench

raised planter
with perennial
planting, grasses
and lavenders

raised lawn

raised planter with
fastigiate hornbeam
trees and grasses

Garden Plan

The garden is to have visual and spatial connectivity with the interior space and the glazed structure. To provide a multifunctional space with semi private areas for sitting, relaxing, socializing and eating and the ability to host functions. Hedges and planting create flexible, semi private seating areas within the garden.

Create a stunning sculptural element, in clearly defined areas for dramatic impact and to draw people into the garden. Provide good circulation within the garden and easy access to all areas. Floating benches provide flexible seating for numerous people and are lit beneath at night.

Create different planes within the garden to help define separate areas. By creating striking horizontal planes which build up in layers - trees, sculptural frames, hedges, planters, lawns, paths, benches are all set at different heights. These changes in level throughout the garden provide greater interest and opportunities for seating. Create numerous changing views within the garden so each space has a different outlook yet is visually linked to the whole garden. Each separate area is unique in size, shape and design and yet all are part of a unified approach. Retain the openness of the garden with the sense of sky and views.

Lighting is paramount as the garden will be used around the clock and is also important during colder weather when the garden will be viewed from inside.

TIPS

Ellen Key
The Century of the Child
Environment plays a very important role on a person's growth, a good environment is the foundation for children to form correct ideas and outstanding personality.

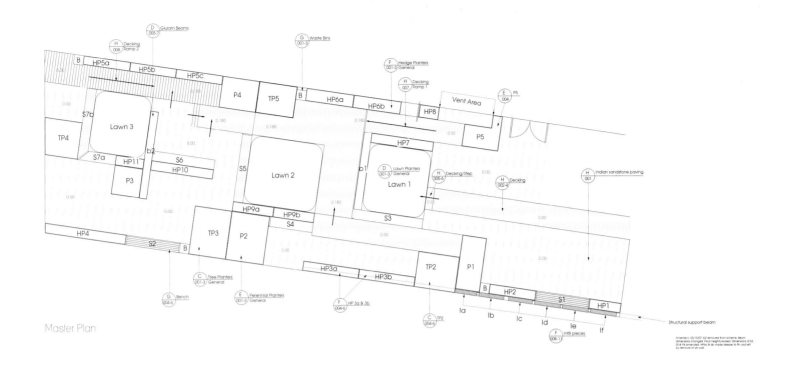

Master Plan

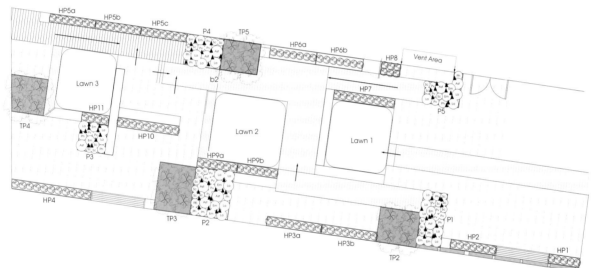

Planting Plan

Song Sheng

COMMENT

Trees, sculptures, fences, laws, various objects piled up have broken the original sequences for a new landscape. Rich colors will greatly meet psychological needs of the children and bring a sense of pleasure and relax experience for visitors. Material changes, scattered plants, interspersed sculptures together have created a lively, free, sensual and intimate social place. Organic combinations of artificial and natural elements with space and height variation offer lots of small spaces connected but not interfering each other. These small places are like private rooms, where people sit in quietly waiting for time running or chatting. Thus they endow the garden with a new lease of life.

COMMUNITY ECOLOGY

"Urban Tropical Rain Forest Feeling"

Skyrise Garden of The Pinnacle Duxton

Landscape Architect: Arc Studio Architecture + Urbanism in collaboration with RSP
Architects Planners & Engineers (Pte) Ltd
Client: Housing & Development Board
Location: Singapore
Site Area: 25,172.1 m²
Cost: SGD $279 million
Photography: Arc Studio Architecture + Urbanism,
RSP Architects Planners & Engineers (Pte) Ltd
Drawings & Plans: Arc Studio Architecture + Urbanism

CLIMATIC CONDITIONS

Singapore belongs to tropical rainforest climate, temperature is hot and humid, the minimum difference in daily and yearly temperature, monthly average temperature 24-27 degrees, annual rainfall is about 2,400 mm, with no typhoon harassment.

PLANTS

broadleaf trees, stonecrop plants, leafy herbaceous plants

DUXTON PLAIN

NEIL ROAD

CANTONMENT ROAD

Site Plan

Soaring at 50-storeys, Pinnacle @ Duxton redefines high-rise high-density living and challenges the conventions of public housing as an architectural typology. The project addresses pragmatic, financial, social issues, and responds sensitively to a myriad of planning constraints. It boldly demonstrates a sustainable and liveable urban high-rise high- density living and initiates an innovative typology of public communal spaces that are metaphorically reclaimed from the air.

The constraints of a tight and irregular-shaped site in the prime central business district area required an efficient and clear block layout that addressed the westerly-facing site. In response, seven tower blocks housing 1,848 apartment units are placed in the most open and porous way, creating urban windows that frame the city skyline. With this manoeuvre, the layout eliminates overlooking between units; optimizes views, connection, air and light flow; minimizes Western exposure to reduce solar heat gain; and retains significant existing trees. A large forecourt for the towers was created, maintaining visual connectivity with the existing Tanjong Pagar Community Club. Residents are well-connected to the transport network and amenities by bus stops and two MRT stations within a 10 minute walking-radius; and enjoy the convenience of shops, food court, education and childcare centres, and a residents' committee centre.

From afar, the building structure stands in the urban greenery, framing the distant blue sky, among the lush trees reveal several conserved red-roofed shop houses in the surroundings. The 1st two floors and basement house the car park and the mechanical & electrical equipment rooms, and the seven housing towers sit on top. The roof of the car park was designed as a roof top garden, with slopes and lush greenery, creating pathways, different spaces for communal activities or for residents to take a break. This roof top garden metaphorically is a new hill.

The new hill is a lush environment deck that connects strategically with the existing urban network while forming a green lung for the city. Layers of tree screens border the site and pathways to provide varying degrees of opacity and privacy, softening the massiveness of the towers.

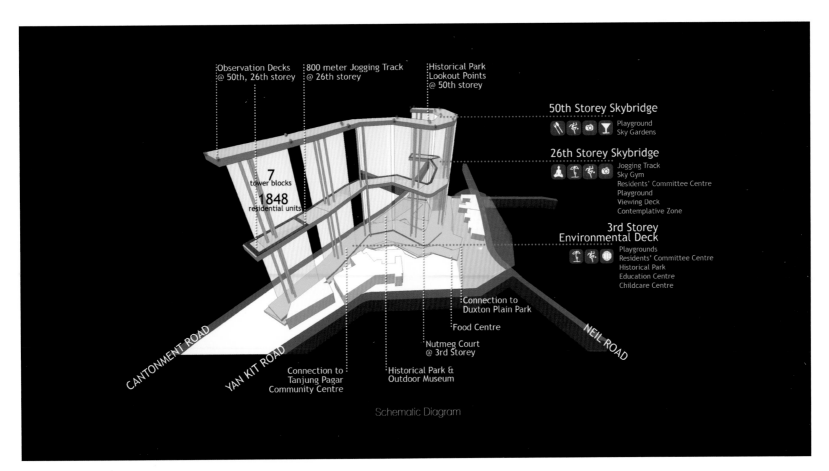

Observation Decks
@ 50th, 26th storey

800 meter Jogging Track
@ 26th storey

Historical Park
Lookout Points
@ 50th storey

50th Storey Skybridge
Playground
Sky Gardens

26th Storey Skybridge
Jogging Track
Sky Gym
Residents' Committee Centre
Playground
Viewing Deck
Contemplative Zone

**3rd Storey
Environmental Deck**
Playgrounds
Residents' Committee Centre
Historical Park
Education Centre
Childcare Centre

7
tower blocks

1848
residential units

Connection to
Duxton Plain Park

Food Centre

Nutmeg Court
@ 3rd Storey

Historical Park &
Outdoor Museum

Connection to
Tanjung Pagar
Community Centre

CANTONMENT ROAD

YAN KIT ROAD

NEIL ROAD

Schematic Diagram

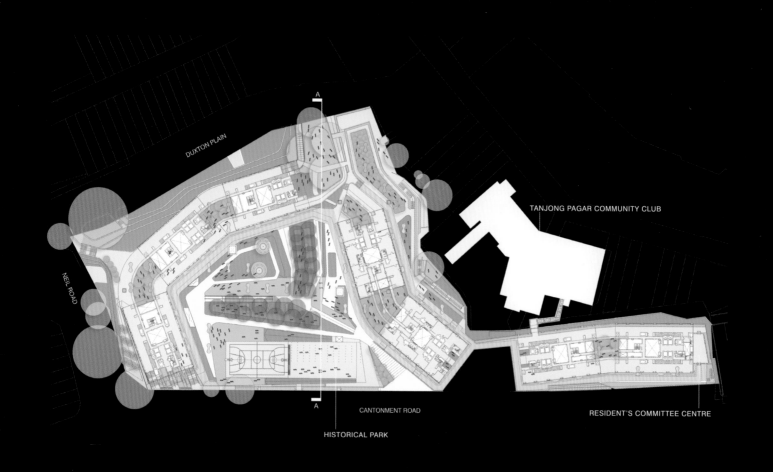

DUXTON PLAIN

TANJONG PAGAR COMMUNITY CLUB

NEIL ROAD

A

A

CANTONMENT ROAD

RESIDENT'S COMMITTEE CENTRE

HISTORICAL PARK

3rd Storey Plan

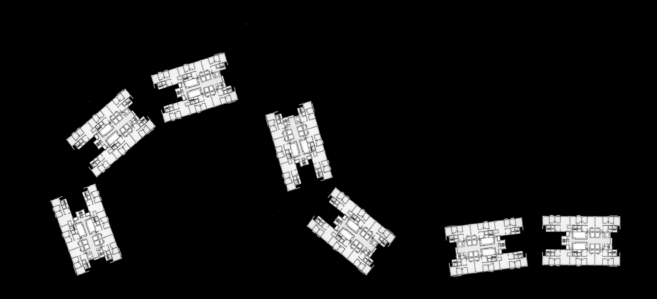

Typical Floor Plan

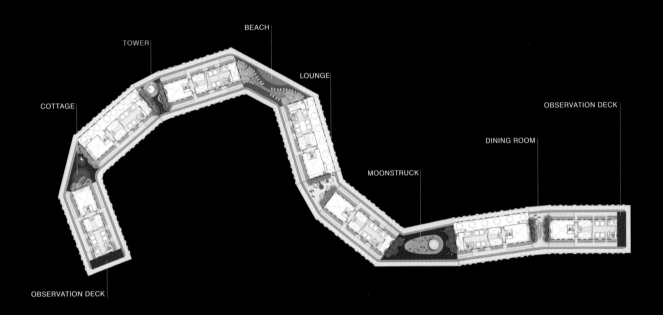

TOWER

BEACH

LOUNGE

COTTAGE

OBSERVATION DECK

DINING ROOM

MOONSTRUCK

OBSERVATION DECK

50th Storey Plan

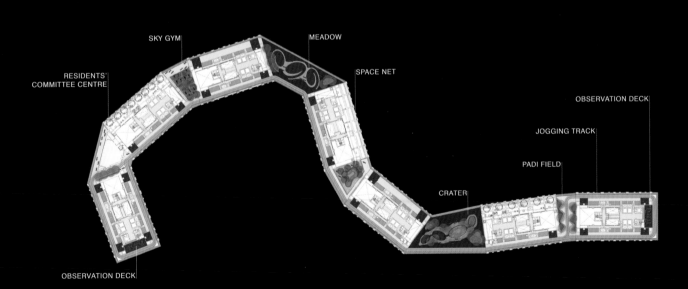

SKY GYM

MEADOW

RESIDENTS'
COMMITTEE CENTRE

SPACE NET

OBSERVATION DECK

JOGGING TRACK

PADI FIELD

CRATER

OBSERVATION DECK

26th Storey Plan

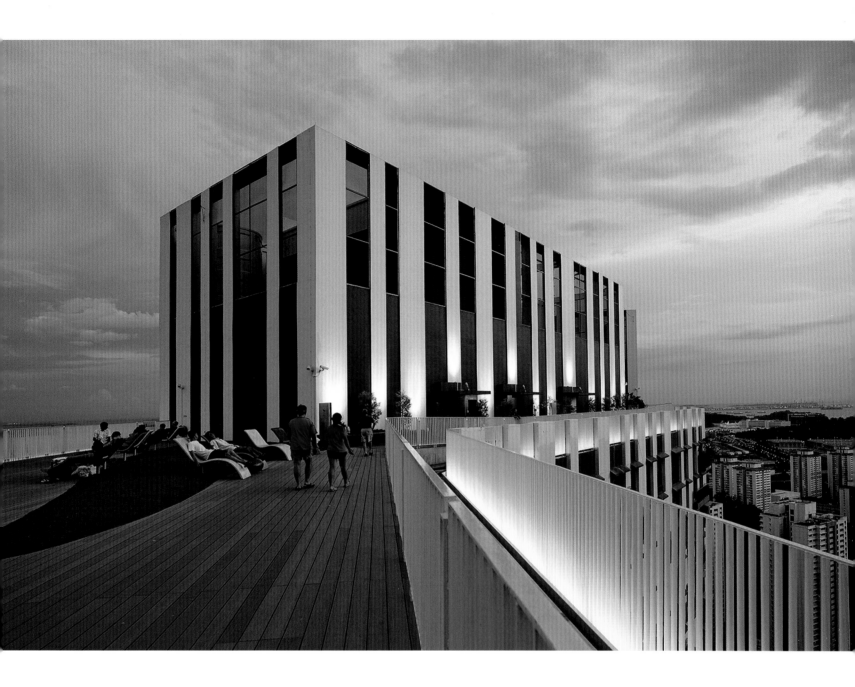

Along the outside the terrace of 26th layer along is fixed with white iron guardrail, there are natural batten floor along inner of terrace, the layer between the wall and terrace are covered with turf. Standing on natural batten with green grass behind, when you take an overlooking on the city landscape, immediately it let a person relaxation fully, relaxing in the bosom of nature.

TIPS

"Bioclimatic Shyscrapers" refers biological climatology applied in high-rise buildings. Mr. Ken Yeang(Contemporary Architects) considered that a building can extend the time without air conditioning and heating equipment to eight and a half months if bioclimatic methods are taken. These buildings with bioclimatology will save more energy cost by electrical equipment than those who did not, which the most desirable place of bioclimatology.

Pang Wei

COMMENT

Located in the high density living "machine", the sky garden tries to melt the alienation among households. Life is like an air travel, it reminds people of the associated with apartment of Marseille of Le Corbusier.

"Cross the busy street, find a sense of belonging."

The Rooftop Garden of QDJCZ Residence

Landscape Architect: Jingsen Landscape Design Co., Ltd
Client: Kunjun Construction Co., Ltd.
Location: Kaohsiung, Taiwan, China
Site Area: 1,652 m²

CLIMATIC CONDITIONS

Taiwan has a high temperature throughout the year, the average annual temperature is above 22 °C. The coldest month is generally above 16 °C in winter. It belongs to the typical tropical monsoon climate.

PLANTS

arbor, shrub, colorful flowers, plumeria, erbatamia divaricata, osmanthus fragrans, common jasmin orange, nandina domestica thunb

EDITOR'S CHOICE

The overall public space seems clean, quiet, natural and elegant. Rich changeable lighting, composition of natural stone texture, contrast of the material's colors, all decrease superfluous decorative elements, but adds a piece of living temperature. Follows the light rhythms, the landscape is as the mysterious light box from the God, to experience low-key luxury fashion.

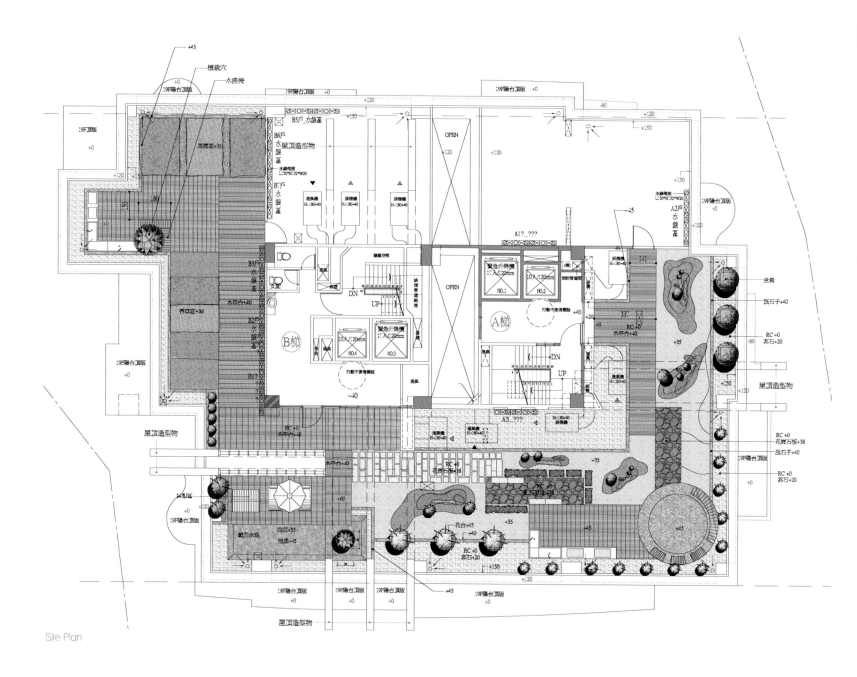

Site Plan

In order to further improve the living quality, people who live in a bustling city should have their own leisure space, tuning out the tumult of the city and shaping the quiet environment for a good mood back home.

Slow down the life pace, form a new campaign for health. This not only provide a leisure purpose for general strolling, but also plant vanilla for health regimen and landscaping, while can have another thinking space to plant private organic flowers tea entertain family and friends.

The design has considered both functions and landscaping to offer users a intimate sense and enjoyment while emphasizing a leisure atmosphere by furnishing decoration and styling. Roof garden has set a vanilla field, meditation area, view platform, barbecue area,

sunbath area and star gym to accommodate community activities for people relaxed and exercise.

The design of Meditation area satisfies the needs of the household. There, it is surrounded by the plantings and water, which are interwoven into a beautiful picture of water and sky at present. Also, the communication place of sky gym adopts the big window and keeps the indoor and outdoor visual effects and the concept of enframed scenery, introducing the greening scenery of sky garden and the beautiful scene of building in the city. In this space of the combination of dynamic and static, as night falls, the warm light is scattered in every corner which makes people who are eager in different activities enjoy the same vivid and rich visual feeling.

TIPS

Health Campaigns

It is the organic combination of the two words "movement" and "health". Doing sports to be healthy, sports are forms, health is the purpose. The forms can be flexible and can be created their freely as long as achieving the purpose of fitness.

The planting part is covered with nearly 20 kinds of arbors, bushes and colorful flowers that are fit for the weather of Kaohsiung, showing different colors level of leaves, texture and flowers. It plans to conduct multi-level plantings filled with diverse color and fragrance, such as plumeria, crepe jasmine, osmanthus, daphne odera and nandina, increasing fragrances and colors changing all the year round.

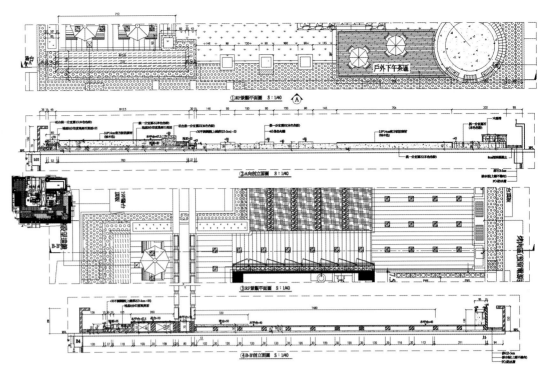

Detailed Drawing 1

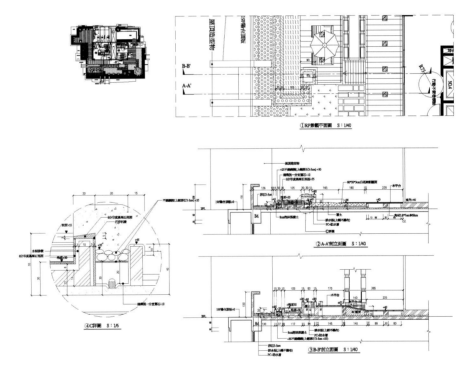

Detailed Drawing 2

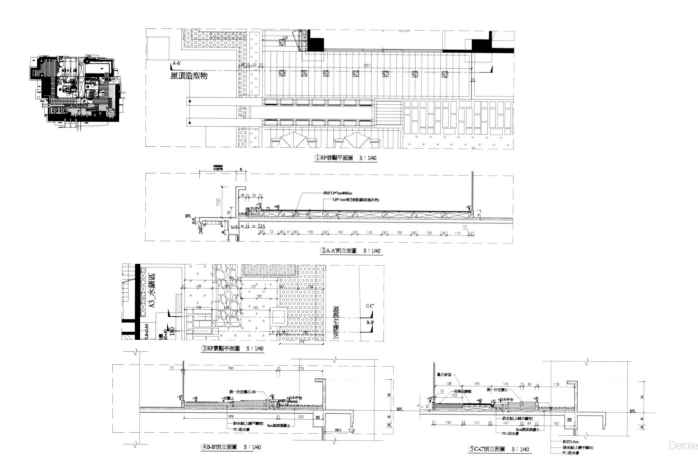

①RF景觀平面圖　S：1/40

②A-A'剖立面圖　S：1/40

③RF景觀平面圖　S：1/40

④B-B'剖立面圖　S：1/40

⑤C-C'剖立面圖　S：1/40

Detailed Drawing 3

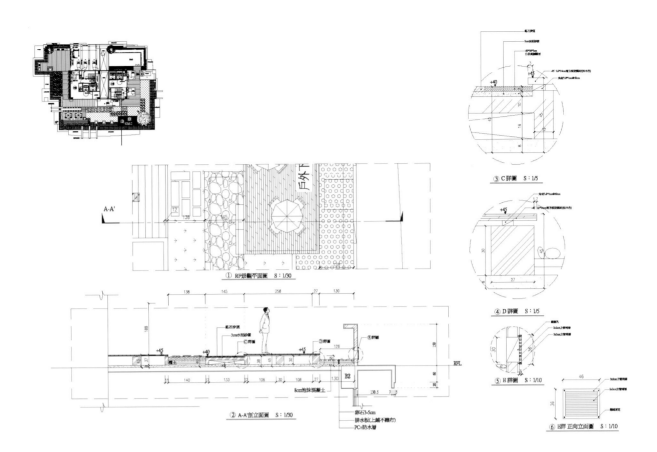

③ C詳圖 S：1/5

④ D詳圖 S：1/5

⑤ E詳圖 S：1/10

⑥ E詳 正向立面圖 S：1/10

① RP景觀平面圖 S：1/30

② A-A'剖立面圖 S：1/30

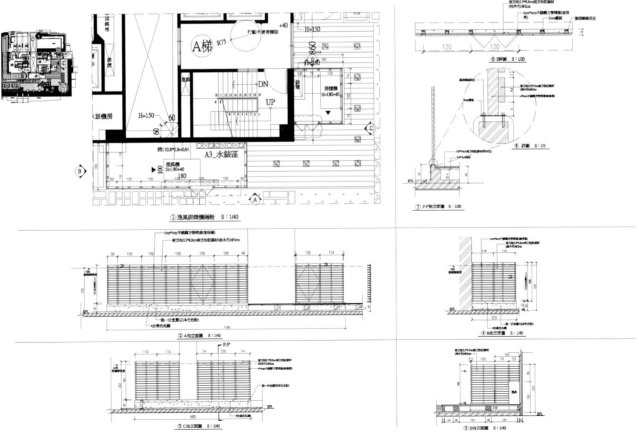

① 進風排煙機柵欄 S：1/40

⑥ E詳圖 S：1/20

⑧ 詳圖 S：1/5

⑦ F-F向立面圖 S：1/20

② A向立面圖 S：1/40

④ B向立面圖 S：1/40

③ C向立面圖 S：1/40

⑤ D向立面圖 S：1/40

The night-time lighting will be properly assigned according to different spatial properties, the using needs and scenery atmosphere, which not only supplies the light for nocturnal activities, but also portrays another kind of landscape different from the scene of the day.

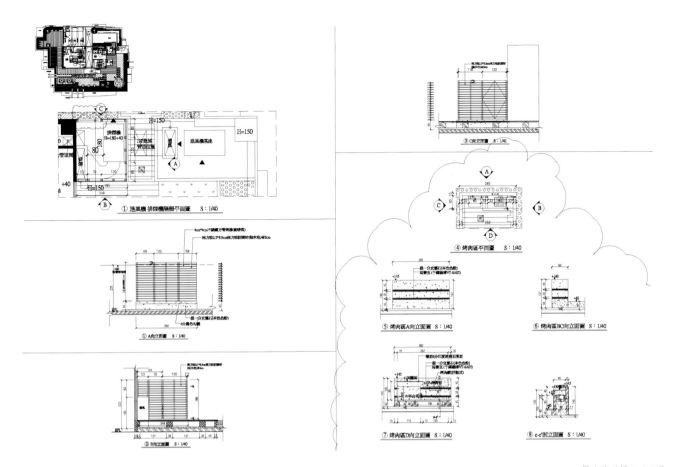

① 送風機 排煙機隔柵平面圖　S：1/40

③ C向立面圖　S：1/40

④ 烤肉區平面圖　S：1/40

① A向立面圖　S：1/40

② B向立面圖　S：1/40

⑤ 烤肉區A向立面圖　S：1/40

⑥ 烤肉區BC向立面圖　S：1/40

⑦ 烤肉區D向立面圖　S：1/40

⑧ c-c剖立面圖　S：1/40

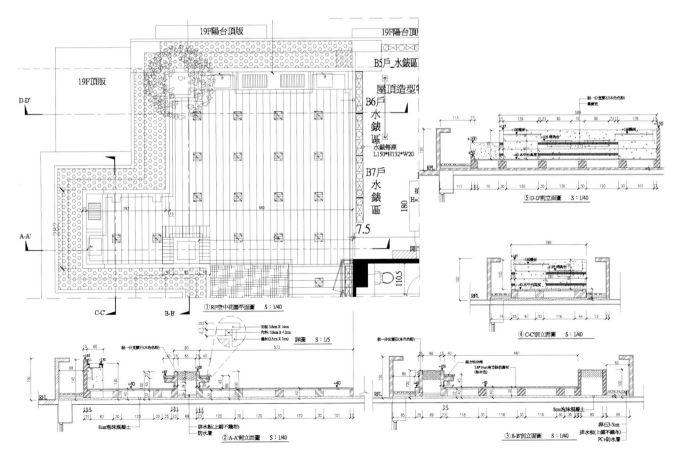

19F陽台頂版

19F陽台頂版

19F頂版

B5戶 水錶區

屋頂造型

B6戶 水錶區

水錶每座
L150*H132*W20

B7戶 水錶區

① RF空中花園平面圖　S：1/40

詳圖　S：1/5

⑤ D-D剖立面圖　S：1/40

④ C-C剖立面圖　S：1/40

② A-A剖立面圖　S：1/40

③ B-B剖立面圖　S：1/40

"Design affects people's daily life; making the environment delightful and good for health is the ambition for a landscape architect."

East Coast

Landscape Architect: Mathews Nielsen Landscape Architects
Client: TF CORNERSTONE
Location: Queens, NY, USA

CLIMATIC CONDITIONS

New York is in temperate continental climate with warm summers and cool winters that leads to a temperature difference in a year. It has concentrated rainfalls in certain periods and four distinct seasons.

PLANTS

pine

EDITOR'S CHOICE

Designers do the overall terrace according to the terrain. The permeable pavement, low-maintain grass, tree pool and seats in geometric lines, and the stone bio-filter pond are well arranged. All these elements show out an effect as the fences disappeared and build out a new stunning landscape on the East River in Manhattan! It also offers variety of entertainment for the residents.

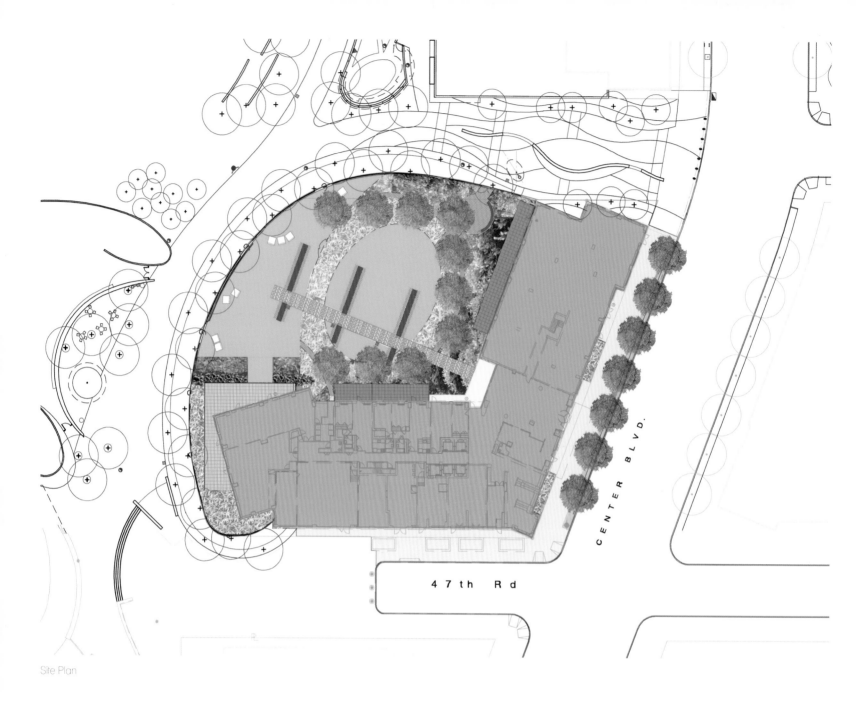

Site Plan

Mathews Nielsen was commissioned to design the private courtyards and streetscapes for six new residential buildings on the former Pepsi site at Queens West. The first building, was completed in 2006, and includes a 3/4 acre open space fronting the waterfront park. The design concept extends the visual experience from the lobby into a physical expression in the landscape where framed views of the Manhattan skyline evolve into an expansive panorama of the East River.

Subtle topographic changes create privacy for the ground floor unit terraces and allow a perimeter fence to visually disappear from inside the courtyard. A variety of sustainable site strategies were incorporated including permeable pavers, no-mow meadows and a rock-lined biofiltration basin. We envisioned a topography of dunes that would create new natural spaces and respond to rooftop conditions. Other outdoor spaces serve more for contemplation and appreciation of their visual beauty. A lobby offers the lovely vista of a mature pine grove. Wide plazas open onto stunning views of Manhattan across the East River.

Each incorporates diverse recreation opportunities for the residents, from areas for grilling and sunbathing to yoga and putting greens and even a bocce court. Many of these activities take place on rooftops that also have innovative plantings of grasses and perennials.

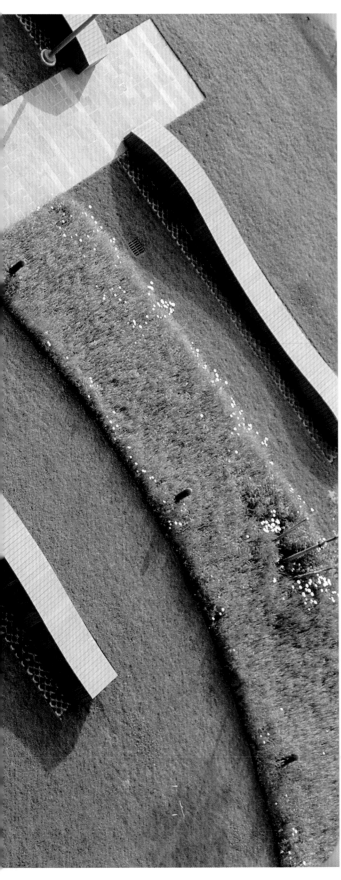

TIPS

Outdoor Public Places

With the development of congregated housing, more and more people began to step into city life. While outdoor public places for congregated housing community are more and more important for people's physical and psychological needs. People in these green areas can have a variety of entertainments, such as barbecue, solarium, exercise (yoga, golf putting green, rolling greens) and other leisure or family activities.

Kim Mathews

COMMENT

Landscape architecture is a profoundly positive and collaborative profession. It is a discipline that embodies hope and requires a longer, larger vision.

"Watch the flowing water, listen to the bird song."

Prive' by Sansiri

Landscape Architect: T.R.O.P terrains + open space
Client: Sansiri Venture Co.Ltd,
Location: Bangkok, Thailand
Site Area: 760 m²
Cost: $ 290,322
Photography: Charkhrit Chartarsa, Pok Kobkongsanti

CLIMATIC CONDITIONS

Bangkok belongs to the typical tropical monsoon climate. Influenced by Asian southwest monsoon and the northeast monsoon, it has high temperature all the year round, small temperature difference, and abundant rainfall.

EDITOR'S CHOICE

The landscape is shaped by a unique design in a luxurious yet low-key atmosphere. The huge infinity pool covers most areas of the garden; the statue wall, sketches and vegetation elaborately embellish of the remaining parts. Every detail hidden in every corner of the garden tells a delicate and elegant feel. It not only makes full use of the existing resources, but also upgrades the ecological design conception into a new sublimation.

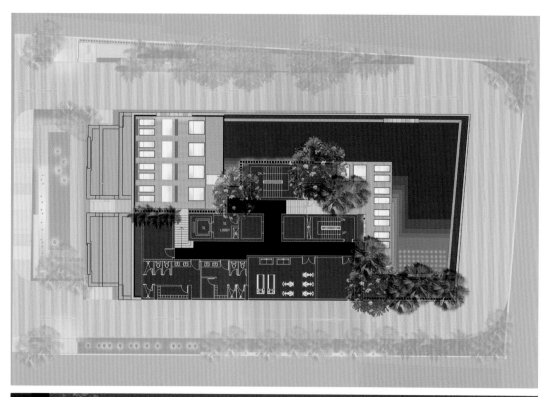

Prive' by Sansiri is an Exclusive Luxury Condominium in the prime Bangkok location. Our target group is a successful 40-plus people, so the design has to be neat and elegant.

TROP's scope includes the Ground Floor Garden and the Swimming Pool on the Roof. For the Ground Floor, Sansiri asked us to create a wall to enclose and screen the Lobby from the public. However, we found that the area is a bit small. So instead of building solid wall, which would make the area feel even smaller, we proposed a custom-designed Sculpture Wall as the alternative. The Wall is a series of Sculptural Columns, each has some space between one another. As the result, the area has some ventilation and plays with natural light in a much more interesting way. At the base of the Columns, we strategically place a Reflecting Pond to make the visual even more beautiful.

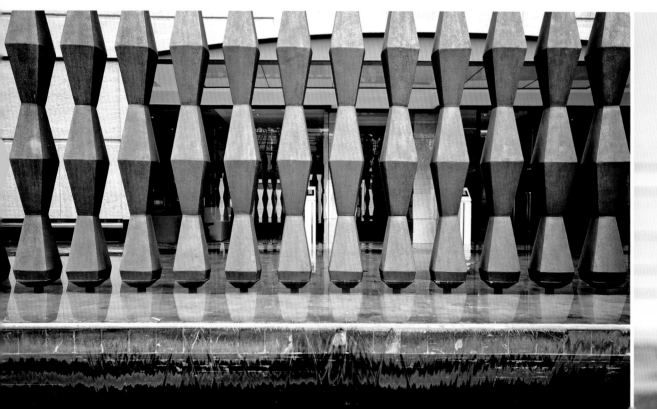

TIPS

Sculpture

In almost all gardens, sculptures are important elements, particularly suitable for rooftop gardens to highlight a feature or create a focal point. But be careful that the weight of sculptures must undergo a rigorous calculation to avoid exceeding the capacity of the roof. If the sculptures are included pools or fountains, the weight of water should be considered with the loading. Materials can be changed if sculptures are overweight: hollow metal and plastic are both good choices.

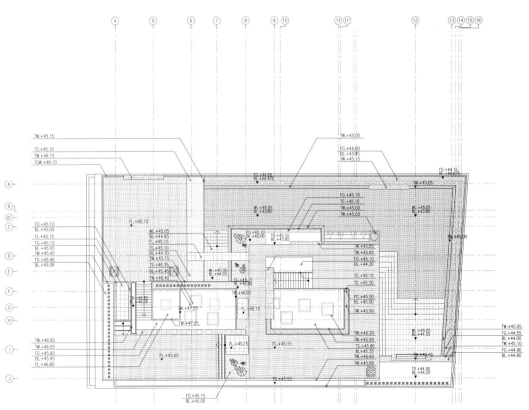

Level Plan

For the Pool, originally, the architect provides a small rectangular pool in the middle of the roof. Because we have a great view here, we suggested them to create an L-Shape Pool, right at the edge of the building instead.

With this design, we have one of the best view of Bangkok for our resident. Then we play with the composition of the Pool Terrace. We divide the Terrace into several portions. This way, a person would not see the whole garden at once. He has to walk around and discover some secret corners in the garden by himself. With a variety of space provided on the roof, everyone can use it without disturbing others.

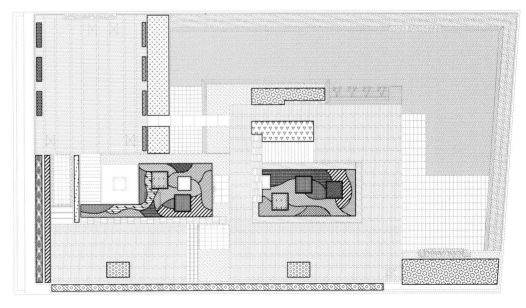

Shrub Plan

Pang Wei

COMMENT

This hotel-like "fine decoration" roof garden means high construction and maintenance costs.

"Bustle fades away with elegance stay."

Rooftop Garden of Ling Xian Residence

Landscape Architect: Jingsen Landscape Design Co., Ltd
Client: Cheng Yang Construction Co., Ltd.
Location: Kaohsiung, Taiwan, China
Site Area: 916 m²

CLIMATIC CONDITIONS

Southern Taiwan has a high temperature all around the year, the average annual temperature is above 22 ℃. The coldest month is generally above 16 ℃ in winter. It belongs to the typical tropical monsoon climate.

EDITOR'S CHOICE

Due to subtropical climate, the project acquires a North-South configuration. Vegetation, ponds, wooden galleries, drying area, lounge, and urban farm turn the roof in the hot southern Taiwan into a rare oasis in the city.

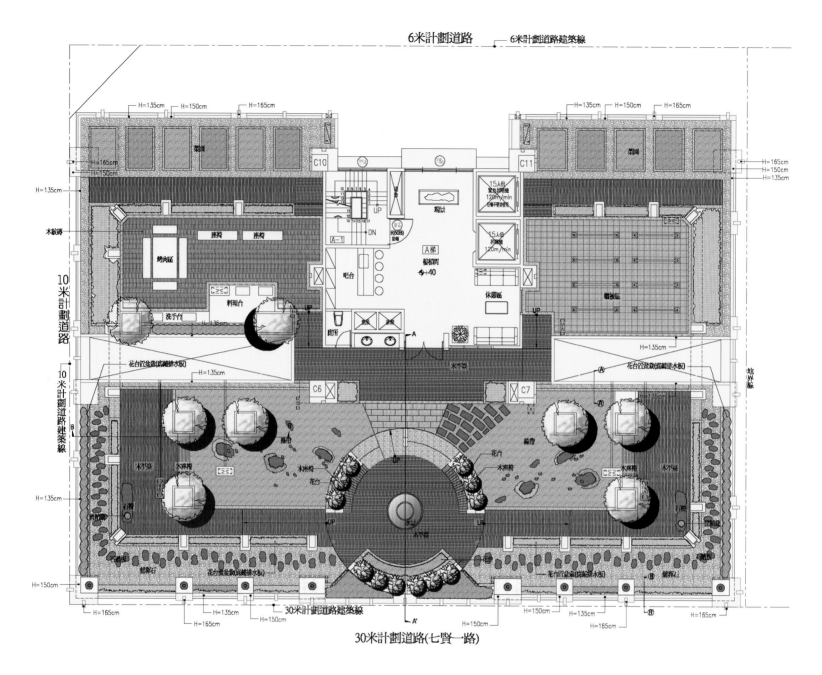

Site Plan

In order to meet subtropical climate, the designer creates a North-South configuration to improve a comfortable and qualified life and achieve an eco-home with functions of energy saving, greenery, and water conservation build on the roof as a roof garden. Shaping the roof as an ecological garden instead of concrete one by strengthening landscape planting, a coherent air green system is constructed with external buildings to make the idea of green space come true.

Light color stones are embedded in decorative tawny glasses to form a contrast, and the minimalist lines dealing with details make the space look more elegant. Air saloon surrounded by greenery, and space materials are on the use of low-saturation colors. Simple lines of the bar counter render the space theme, the ceiling and the meticulous lamps and lanterns beside the elevator entrance bring out low-key costly sense lightly. Specially processed gallery façade makes the functional space combined with the façade ingeniously.

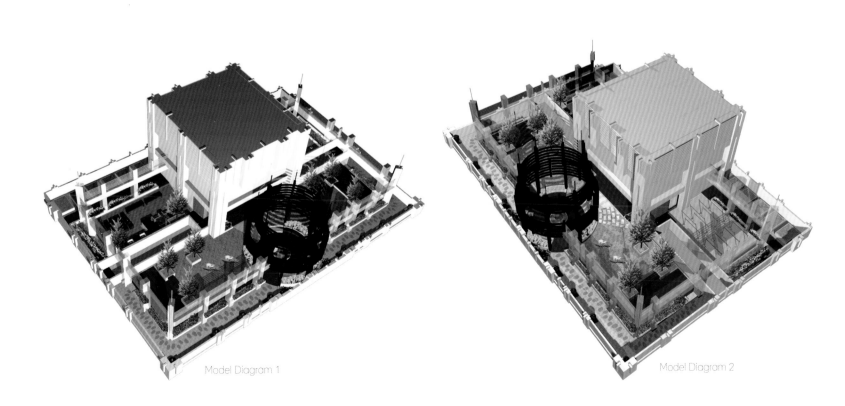

Model Diagram 1

Model Diagram 2

The community roads set in natural patterns in the atrium provide a static yet dynamic space. There is an open community plaza in the central part where is shaped of styling furniture, the pool is as the centre beside it, creating a visual focus in the atrium. Walking under the delicate wooden corridor will come to the axial recreation area, on both sides of the rooftop terrace, one is as the drying area, and the other is the outdoor dining area, providing a good space for barbecue party. The atrium concentrates natural imagery as the courtyard landscape essence and introduces it to interior space. The fences as crude interfaces between half exterior and half interior spaces are broken to be a smooth one.

Setting the urban farm-garden and vanilla garden at terrace space on both sides of the rooftop provides the fun of planting by oneself and an open space for enjoyment. While in the hot southern Taiwan, large areas of green spaces are a rare seem oasis in the city.

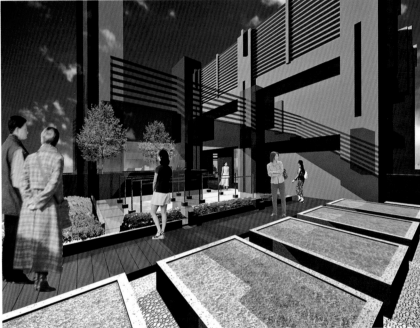

TIPS

Rooftop Farming
Rooftop farming is now common in urban areas, where ground-level agricultural opportunities are scarce. is a specialty in urban planning. Rooftop farms absorb solar radiation to relief 'urban heat island effect', insulates and cools the main building (and thereby reduces electricity use), and manage stormwater by delaying and reducing. The manifold benefits of rooftop farming are exciting, proven, and available now.

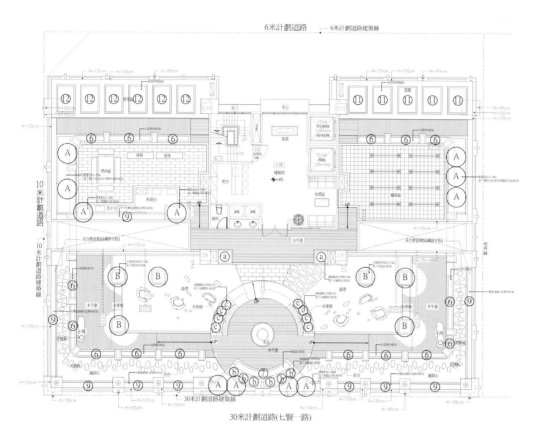

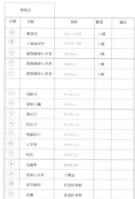

Plant Layout

"A Fallen Wish"

Do Ho Suh Fallen Star

Landscape Architect: Spurlock Poirier Landscape Architects
Location: San Diego, California, USA

CLIMATIC CONDITIONS

San Diego is located in southern California, USA, which is not too cold all the year round although it is near the sea.

PLANTS

purple flowering plum, fortunei 'green lane', wax-leaf privet, golden berberis, juniperus, conferta 'blue pacific', buddleja alternifolia (fountain butterfly bush), parthenocissus quinquefolia (virginia creeper), lonicera japonica 'halliana' (hall's honeysuckle)

EDITOR'S CHOICE

Artists and technical team have transformed the existing roof and parapet wall to solve the loading problem. The cantilevered-supported ectopic house will make this New England village-style roof garden far more fascinating.

Spurlock Poirier had a unique, collaborative role in this site installation for the Stuart Collection. The artwork explores ideas of home, dislocation and relocation. Working with the artist Do Ho Suh, SPLA devised a strategy for creating a New England cottage garden on the 7th floor roof of the Jacobs.

This interface becomes a sustainable strategy that aims to maximize biodi¬versity and sustainable design in this urban site by extending green space both horizontally and vertically within the renovated apartment and exterior roof space. The result, hypernature, is an artificial spectacle of constructed nature. Natural forms and phenomena are revealed and re-visioned into a magical landscape for living. Ecology and art meet at the surface creating an explosion of life within the urban context.

The landscape concept was to recreate a residential garden that is informal, inviting, somewhat ad hoc and even artless, using with plants that would be typically found in Providence, Rhode Island, the artist's previous home. To that end, we selected plants that grow in the northeast as well as southern California, are commonly found in residential gardens and retail nurseries and are tolerant of coastal and windy conditions. Plants included Prunus cerasifera (Purple Flowering Plum), a ubiquitous spring-flowering accent tree; vigorous, reliable screening shrubs such as Euonymus fortunei 'Green Lane' and Ligustrum japonicum 'Texanum' (Wax-leaf Privet) for background screening of the parapet walls, guard rails, irrigation controllers and other rooftop equipment and generally giving a sense of enclosure. Smaller, more compact ornamental shrubs including Berberis thunbergii 'Aurea' (Golden Berberis) and Juniperus conferta 'Blue Pacific' that are popular, low-maintenance and often used to add accent and texture to residential yards; Buddleja alternifolia (Fountain Butterfly Bush) For color and contrast, used as a single specimen; a variety of vines, including Parthenocissus quinquefolia (Virginia Creeper) and Lonicera japonica 'Halliana' (Hall's Honeysuckle), intended to train along the guardrails and even creep onto the house itself.

TIPS

Roof garden loads includes: 1, the planting area loads; 2, flower beds and potted plants loads; 3, garden water engineering loads; 4, the rockery and sculpture loads; 5, garden ornaments and landscape architecture loads.

COMMENT

Zhang Wenying

The cantilevered house breaks the limitation of the common square roof and broadens the garden visually. The plant configuration is a critical factor in the design. Low shrubs featured in sea wind and drought resisting not only alleviate loading but also make the garden seem larger. Flowering, climbing and paving plants are chosen from native vegetation in CA, combined with the undulating terrain, huts, winding trails and grass together, perfectly capturing the style of England countryside homes.

"Modern Inheritance Of Ancient Civilization."

Rooftop Gardens in 24 solar terms Gardens

Landscape Architect: EARTHSCAPE
Client: Mitsui Fudosan Residential
Location: Tokyo, Japan
Site Area: 28,900 m²

CLIMATIC CONDITIONS

Tokyo has a temperate maritime monsoon climate with four distinct seasons and abundant rainfall. Influenced by southeast monsoon, there is more rain in summer but less snow in winter.

PLANTS

reed

EDITOR'S CHOICE

The project offers such unique creativity that it brings the tradition of 24 solar terms into the design. Each garden has a crowning touch emphasizing characteristics of each solar term. The old traditional features integrated with modern garden design to point out a road for both parties in contemporary landscape design.

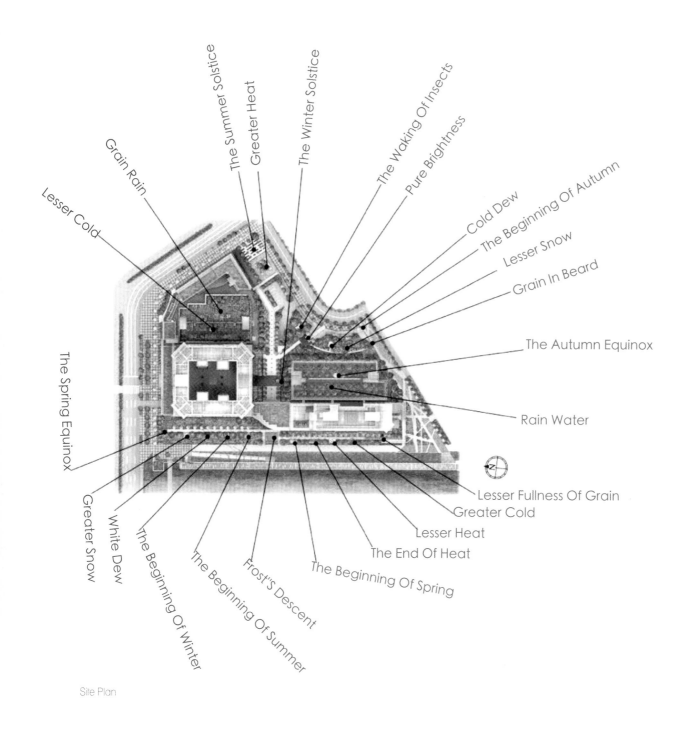

Grain Rain

Lesser Cold

The Summer Solstice

Greater Heat

The Winter Solstice

The Waking Of Insects

Pure Brightness

Cold Dew

The Beginning Of Autumn

Lesser Snow

Grain In Beard

The Spring Equinox

The Autumn Equinox

Rain Water

Greater Snow

White Dew

The Beginning Of Winter

Frost''S Descent

The Beginning Of Summer

The Beginning Of Spring

The End Of Heat

Lesser Heat

Greater Cold

Lesser Fullness Of Grain

Site Plan

The traditions and aesthetic sensibility of the Japanese people have been fostered through the unique climate of the four seasons in Japan. For this project, we focused on Japanese solar terms as the main concept for the landscape design project at Park City Toyosu. Solar terms are   seasons of approximately 15 days, based on a system of 24 seasons a year beginning at   Setsubun, the traditional end of winter. In times when the lunar calendar was used, solar terms were considered indications for learning the essence of the seasons. Japan is uniquely positioned to experience the luxury of such slight changes in the four seasons. Aiming for a landscape that could be "used," as opposed to just seen, we created 24 private gardens and added various features.

Rain water: Around February 19. It gets warm when snow changes to rain and ice begins to be melted. Winter to spring is the main theme of the garden. Low bushes is planted in the round laws in the garden, which the designer deliberately chooses the color of fresh green to highlight the advent of spring. The brightest spot is a circular field inlaid with letters of "0218". It declares the season of spring rain is coming.

A utumnal equinox: Around Sep 23. The mid of autumn. Autumn is the season of harvest. For this theme, the large area in the garden is covered with grass flourishing or withered dotted with a few low shrubs. This means a transition between new and old, flourishing or withered. With Some higher reeds a cool autumn atmosphere is created. The white circular finishing hidden in the plants is a bright point in the garden.

Slight cold: Around Jan 6. It is rather cold. To show things got depressed in the winter, there are only several square grass fields in the garden with a single pallet, which symbolize the sleeping nature. Staggered in the middle of the grass fields are square wood boards, one of which is painted in striking white color with a hollowed cross-shape. Next to it is a thick white cross, which will be completed with the white board as a puzzle. The depressed tone of grey plants and quiet white board together show the meaning of an old saying: A timely snow promises a good harvest.

COMMENT

Zhang Wenying

Solar terms are a kind of supplemental calendar used for farming guiding originated in China agricultural era. They reflect the movement of the earth around the sun and are important symbols of seasonal changes in a year. The project shows 24 solar terms by means of landscape in 24 gardens, which delivers profound messages and well inherits ancient oriental culture. However, viewers may not understand the implication straightforwardly without appropriate commentary system in the gardens.

"New Renaissance Garden of Life Aesthetics "

Rooftop Garden of Mucha Four Seasons

Landscape Architect: Liu Kuo Landscape Co., Ltd.
Client: Huanbang Construction Co., Ltd.
Location: Taipei, Taiwan, China
Site Area: 3,646.5 m²

CLIMATIC CONDITIONS

Taipei belongs to the subtropical monsoon climate, the annual average temperature is 22.4 °C, annual rainfall is more than 2,100 mm. From July to September is the rainy season, during which the precipitation occupies two-fifths of a year.

EDITOR'S CHOICE

Light color wood matches well with glass walls, showing a harmony with gray stone pillars. The symbioses of empty and full between materials, the contrast of colors, all to decrease fussy decorations and add a low-key liberality.

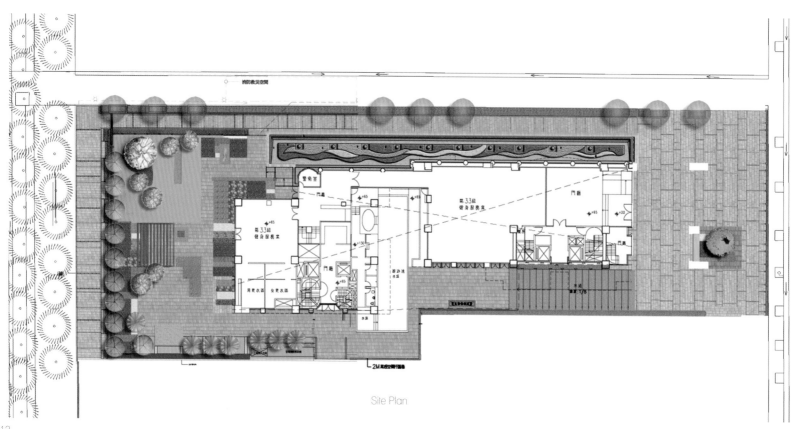

Site Plan

The original design treats the garden of Piet Mondrian as concepts, through leaf shape and texture of various plants, multi-layered planting, flooring patterns, furnishings and wooden gallery frame, rendering the value of Mondrian garden.

In an overall sense, the project uses simple and modern architectural vocabulary. The overall space is an open with purely decorative lines matched with wooden floor to shape an exquisite luxury textures appeal to senses. Woods in light color against the glass walls has formed a contrast and heighten thespace texture by minimalist lines, highlighting the strong artistic temperament.

Simple appearance configuration blended into the new ornamentation style, makes the building present the interlaced texture of modern and classic. Lines extended horizontally shape humanities which implied in graceful temperament. Refined sense of the overall style embodies delicate design elements, and through the interaction of material and low-key colors to show the garden's character and rich appearance that should have people linger on.

Rendering 1

Detailed plan depends on on the simple neat geometry, creating a comfortable open space, a comfortable breathing space, which becomes the excellent performance stage for waterscape, greenery planting and sculptures, and produces a hybrid symbiosis environment.

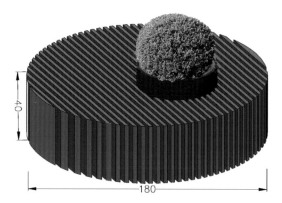

40

180

TIPS

The new ornamentation
The new ornamentation is different from the luxuriant feeling of traditional ornamentation, in that decoration emphasizes the mix of red blossoms and green leaves focuses on practical, elegance and good taste. To show a luxurious sense in simple lines by a mix of different materials, the new ornamentation works toward "humanization" manifestations.

Zhang Wenying

COMMENT

The carefully chosen materials, such as timber, stones, glass and potteries have formed a contrast and highlighted the unique charm of texture. Some simple and clean geometric objects make the garden appear distinctive, sophisticated, filled with an overall sense. Potteries and planters, square or round wooden benches, all like sculptures bring a sense of zen, contributing to a quiet and pure rooftop recreational space, in which shadows are also one of the constituent elements.

"Oh, Sporting on Rooftop!"

Penthouses and Rooftop Terrace

Landscape Architect: JDS+BIG, EKJ
Client: A/B Birkegade
Location: Copenhagen, Denmark
Site Area: 900 m²
Cost: € 950 000
Photography: JDS Heechan Park

CLIMATIC CONDITIONS

Denmark is in temperate marine climate. It is comfortable during the summer with the temperatures in between 22-26 ℃ and the night is cool of 12-18 ℃.

PLANTS

grass, durant vegetation

EDITOR'S CHOICE

An open public space is created by transforming a narrow space. The roofs on the three buildings are planned to be a practical hanging garden, containing a sports lounge, grassy slope park area and sunshine corridors.

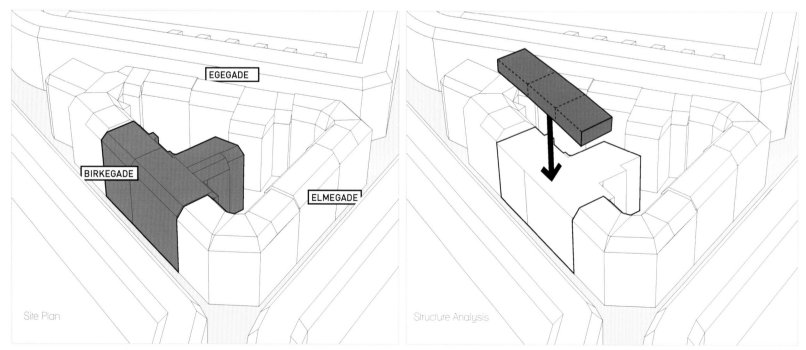

EGEGADE

BIRKEGADE

ELMEGADE

Site Plan

Structure Analysis

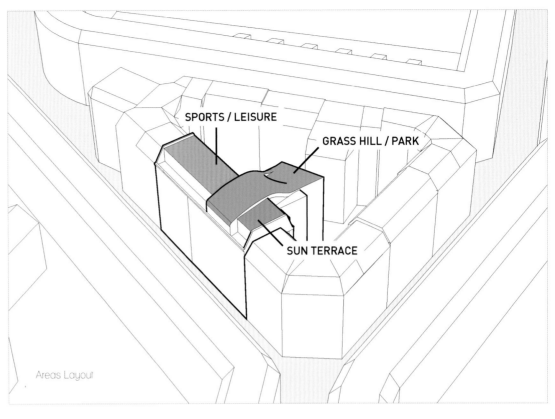

SPORTS / LEISURE

GRASS HILL / PARK

SUN TERRACE

Areas Layout

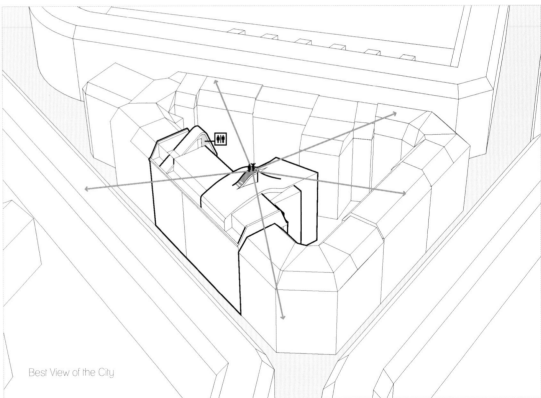

Best View of the City

Elmegade district is probably one of the most densely populated areas of inner Norrebro, CPH. Especially the triangular block Birkegade / Egegade / Elmegade has a very high density, which is reflected in very narrow courtyards.

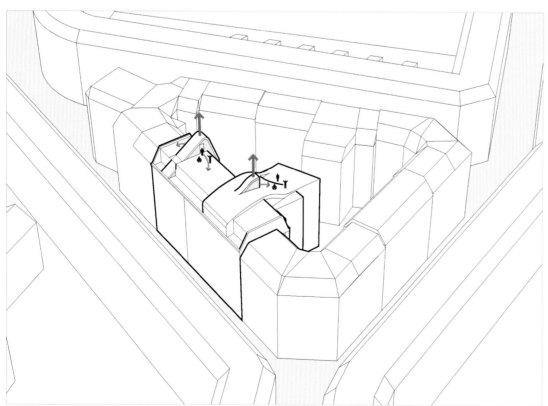

Access

And it is precisely around the cramped courtyard that the concept for BIR originates. The driving concept is to create the 'missing garden' at the top of the existing housing block in association with 3 new penthouses, so all residents gain access to a genuine outdoor garden.

This is reflected in a playground with shock-absorbing surface and a playful suspension bridge, a green hill with varying accommodation backed by real grass and durant vegetation, a viewing platform, an outdoor kitchen and barbecue, and a more quiet wood deck.

The concept for the BIR, is to optimize and fully exploit the situations the site has to offer, and thereby design a potential for the future exploitation of the roof to the delight of all the co-op's residents. It is a concept which is not limited to establish the 3 new apartments, but a concept which both creates a useful roof garden as well as a beautiful landscape for the co-op's neighbours and city residents in general. Usually a roof defines a final measure of any construction – closure. The Birkegade roof opens up for a versatile stay and experience.

TIPS

Roof Stadiums
There are many this kind of projects from worldwide now.

COMMENT

The project has provided residents an outdoor activity spaces free from outside interference by its rich functional areas. Flexible playground, outdoor kitchen and BBQ area, grassy slope and wooden platform offer spaces and areas for sports, socializing and scenery enjoying. This practical kind of rooftop garden will become an integral part for people, integrated in all aspects of daily lives.

Zhang Wenying

PRIVATE ROOFTOP

"Greenery Displays A Modern Nature."

Small Modernist Garden

Landscape Architect: Paul Dracott msgd
Location: Cambridge UK
Site Area: 500 m²
Cost: £ 48,000
Photography: Paul Dracott
Plant: Amelanchier lamarkii, Hebe pinguifolia 'Pagei', Lonicera pileata, Taxus baccata

CLIMATIC CONDITIONS

UK is in temperate marine climate, warm in winter and cool in summer with small temperature difference. It rains throughout the year, especially in winters.

PLANTS

Amelanchier lamarkii, Hebe pinguifolia 'Pagei', Lonicera pileata, Taxus baccata

EDITOR'S CHOICE

The clients admired many styles of garden including Japanese and Persian but the over style was to be modernist. Contemporary furniture by Charles E and other Bauhaus designers set the tone for the final style of the garden as it should be in perfect harmony with the interior.

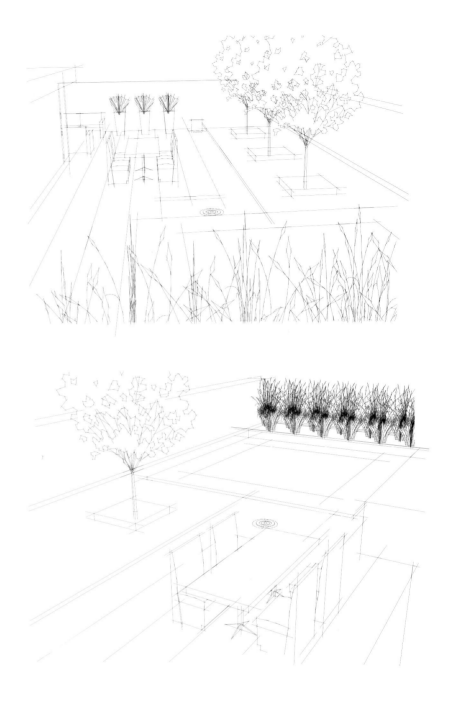

Plan at different parts

The new open plan living space was enclosed totally with a glass wall of sliding doors. As the garden was now viewed almost as part of the interior, the design had to flow out from the glass doors and look fabulous for twelve months of the year. The design solution was to create a large terrace level with the interior flooring and separate the planting from this terrace by a large rill running across the garden. The terrace was paved in a diamond cut grey sandstone. The rill was given movement by a water blade at one end and by a small bubble fountain at the other. The resulting ripples reflecting upon the ceiling of the extension on sunny days.

The planting was restricted to three standard Amelanchier trees in small aluminium raised beds and under planted with a grey hebe. A small raised lawn of course bladed blue alpine turf was edged in large sandstone paving and seems to float above one end of the rill. Planting was completed by a yew hedge in a rendered raised bed to the rear of the garden and shrubby honisuckles clipped into cloud forms.

To maintain the minimalist appearance and prevent flow back into the house, a concealed surface water drainage system was installed, allow efficient surface water drainage with no visual impact.

The color scheme for the materials was shades of grey, pale grey paving contrasted by the darker grey walls. This gave the garden an overwhelming feeling of calm and linked with the window and doors on the house.

Garden lighting was essential as no window dressings were planned for the glass wall. Uplighters for the trees give a sculptural effect with submersible lighting in the rill highlighting the movement of the water. Strip lighting beneath the edge of the raised lawn enhances the illusion that it is floating.

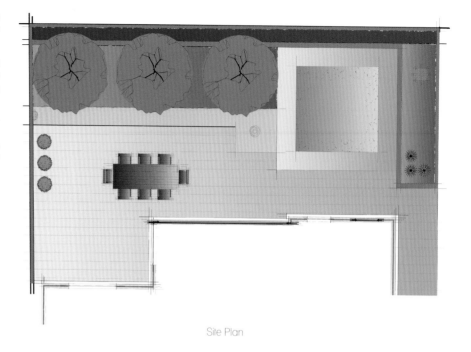

Site Plan

TIPS

Bauhaus
The most important influence on Bauhaus was modernism, a cultural movement which originated as far back as the 1880s. One of the main objectives of Bauhaus was to unify art, craft and technology. It was considered a positive element, and therefore became an important part for industrial and product design.

COMMENT

Despite the simplicity of this design, the project included an extensive concealed surface water drainage and collection system. This protected the rill from contamination and prevented ingress of water to the interior from the exterior surfaces, which were laid at the same level.

Paul Dracott

"Facing the sea with spring blossoms."

Seaside Rooftop Garden

Landscape Architect: Merilen Mentaal - MentaalLandscapes
Client: Private client
Location: Tallinn, Estonia
Site Area: 200 m²
Cost: Over $ 130, 000
Photography: Merilen Mentaal

CLIMATIC CONDITIONS

Tallinn has cold and wet winters (down to -25° C) and cool summers (up to 28° C) with prevailing western winds.

PLANTS

Juniperus communis 'Hibernica', Nepeta faassenii 'Walker's Low', Lavandula angustifolia, Echinacea purpurea 'Alba'

EDITOR'S CHOICE

To meet the requirements of the owner, the garden is divided into different functional areas. Taking full advantage of seashore location, each area is endowed with its unique characteristics by matching seaside plants in cold colors with Indian handcraft furniture in warm colors that ultimately contribute to a leisure garden in a sweet atmosphere.

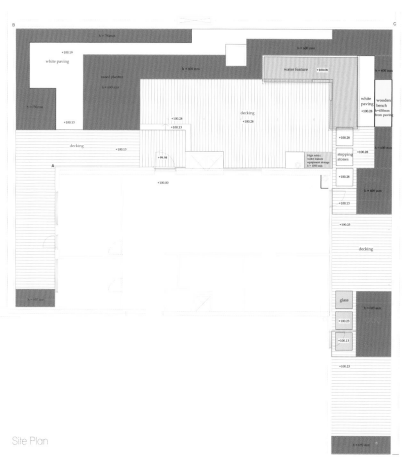

Site Plan

This garden situates right on the beach, on top of a large modern apartment building, backed by a strip of pine forest. The owner is a busy executive who asked for an outdoor entertaining area, a small private garden to have the morning coffee and an herb corner.

The design borrowed the modern features of the house, combined it with all-year-round greenery and added a bit of Asian touch to reflect the interior of the apartment which has similar feeling.

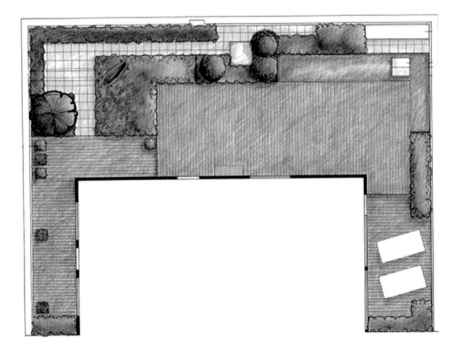

coloured sketch plan of the rooftop garden

Designing the garden, five different areas were created – a morning side garden with large planter for herbs and 3 solitary high planters, which is viewed from the office; lush, paved garden area surrounded by junipers and perennial planting, for to enjoy the morning coffee; the main entertaining terrace to where the main door opens; evening, seaside side-garden which leads to the last side-garden which has more reflective feeling, with an Indian bench and bamboo, viewed from the bedroom.

The entertaining area is quite large, with an L-shape, shallow, reflecting water-feature, a seaside white bench and a simple counter to serve the drinks. The counter, in fact, is a storage place of the water feature equipment. As the weight on the roof had to be as light as possible, the water feature was built of Styrofoam and water-proofed thereafter, finished with large black granite slabs.

3-D View - water feature

Requirements for the materials were maximum durability, therefore the planters and decking is hardwood Cumaru. The color scheme of the design was kept to black (granite) and white (reconstituted granite), with red wood and cold color-scheme planting, except two seaside planters which enjoy the beautiful evening sunsets. The little garden area is a paved square surrounded by lush planting, with white paved floor. The same white paving is in between the bench and the water feature while the rest of the garden spaces have decking on two different levels as flooring. Three large squares stepping stones of white reconstituted granite and another three of glass lit below, lead from the bedroom terrace to the main terrace.

The furniture and few exotic planters are simple wood-carved handcraft products that were brought from India and mixed well with the contemporary feel of the garden.

The planting was kept simple but bold and lush with less maintenance need must. Leading colours are blues and purples together with greens to tie the rooftop with surrounding pines and to present a beach feeling.

Hand Drawing for Planters

TIPS

Color Coordination

Refering to to the color scheme in the garden, it is not only limited to plants, water, soil, rock, roof, grey tone of the urban forest, changing sky and neon lights. Everything viewed on the roof shall be taken into account. However, over-coordination may lead to a blurred or boring effect, which causes boredom or discomfort with long time eyes on it. Therefore, color coordination should provide colorful group with irritation, attractive but not dazzling.

COMMENT

Rooftop gardens are rather unpredictable as they have their own micro-climates that may differ from the conditions below. Everything around that garden influence that micro-climate. This particular garden enjoys few degrees warmer and milder temperature, a lot of sunshine and benefits from the almost direct contact with the sea and therefore becomes lush within a year from its construction and planting. Being partially protected with clear glass railings, the plants grow well beneath.
Other roof-top gardens may face a lot harsher conditions than on the ground and may require more winter-hardy plants to survive living on top of a building.

Merilen Mentaal

"The Habitat of Happiness"

Carnegie Hill House

Landscape Architect: Nelson Byrd Woltz Landscape Architects
Location: Manhattan, New York, USA
Photography: Eric Piasecki

CLIMATIC CONDITIONS

The climate of New York is generally mild with four well-defined seasons. Spring is occasionally struck by showers and the temperature in winter is often below zero Celcius with snowfall.

PLANTS

boston ivy, gingko tree, black locust, leucothoe, ferns, teak, athyrium, iberis, basil, rosemary, sage, thyme, birch, strawberries

EDITOR'S CHOICE

The seasonal vegetation adapting to the dynamic changes of environment, rattan sofa under the ginkgo, boston ivy on the teak fence, purple fern beside the slate road and black locust in line. these well organized elements as a whole are like a elegant and tranquil 3D oil painting.

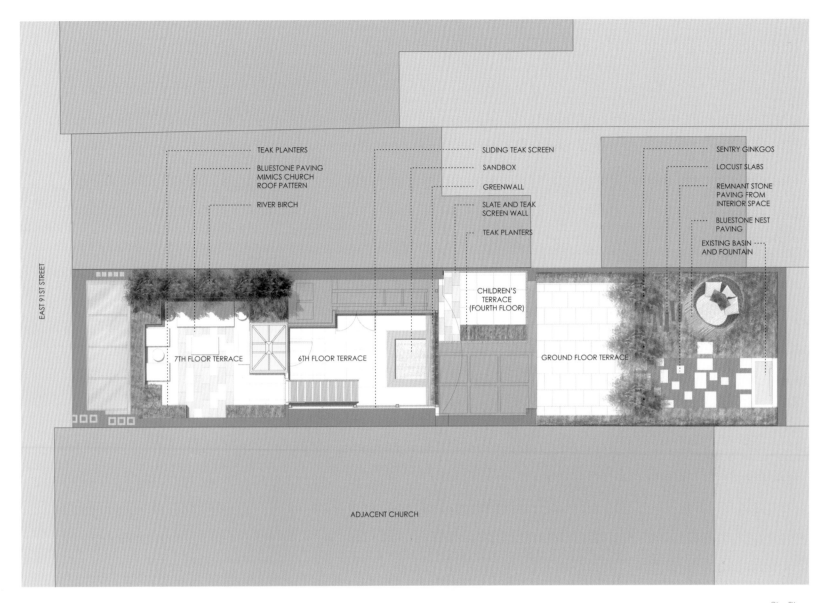

TEAK PLANTERS

BLUESTONE PAVING
MIMICS CHURCH
ROOF PATTERN

RIVER BIRCH

SLIDING TEAK SCREEN

SANDBOX

GREENWALL

SLATE AND TEAK
SCREEN WALL

TEAK PLANTERS

SENTRY GINKGOS

LOCUST SLABS

REMNANT STONE
PAVING FROM
INTERIOR SPACE

BLUESTONE NEST
PAVING

EXISTING BASIN
AND FOUNTAIN

EAST 91ST STREET

7TH FLOOR TERRACE

6TH FLOOR TERRACE

CHILDREN'S
TERRACE
(FOURTH FLOOR)

GROUND FLOOR TERRACE

ADJACENT CHURCH

Site Plan

The planting plan reflects a range of microclimates, from a shaded ground floor terrace, a sheltered children's 'teaching' terrace on the middle floor, and two adjoining terraces on the top floors that are exposed to harsh sunlight and wind. The annual life cycles of the plants create a dynamic environment year-round, and introduce seasonally conditioned places of play and repose for both child and adult.

The ground floor terrace is a lush, five-sided green cube that admits light from above and creates a rich and serene extension of the house's primary living space. Plants indigenous to the woodland understory thrive in the shaded garden floor, while boston ivy climbs up the garden walls and envelopes the space. A line of sentry Gingko trees creates a screen between inside and out, which adds spatial depth, and frames a two-part composition as viewed from inside the house. On one side of the garden diptych, a re-circulating marble fountain enhances the immersive experience of the garden while simultaneously providing water for birds and insects. On the other side, a literal nest is created for the family: black locust sleepers lead to an oversized woven chair that sits low to the ground, surrounded by verdant leucothoe, ostrich ferns, and lady ferns — plants that were discovered on-site during an initial site visit, stored during construction, and replanted.

The upper garden terraces are perched atop the townhouse. Forestry Stewardship Council Certified teak screening is the primary strategy for both defining space and managing the relationship between these garden terraces and their urban surroundings. The design of the teak screens—the result of a close collaboration between the designer and the craftsman—takes figurative cues from the function and qualities of birds' nests. Careful stacking and spacing of teak slats and the subtle and intermittent articulation in the face of the teak imitate the woven quality of a bird's nest and create interplay of light and shadow. Whenever possible throughout the project, existing materials were refreshed and reused. A floating staircase provides passage between the upper terraces. The existing steel stringers were preserved and given new life with the addition of a teak handrail, stainless steel cables, and bluestone treads.

On the roof terraces, the teak screen walls choreograph the experiential relationship between a calm domestic environment and its dense and active urban surroundings. Along the east wall of the 6th floor terrace, a sliding panel opens to frame the adjacent church spire. On sunny summer mornings, the sliding panel closes to provide much-needed shade. The screen wall along the north side of this terrace thickens to embrace a green wall, editing out the buildings beyond and defining a private enclosure scaled to the terrace. Rather than conceived of as an ecological panacea, the greenwall is both artwork and an opportunity for research. The designer and contractor engaged in a trial and error period to determine how best to establish the greenwall plants; much like a framed painting, Athyrium, Gualtheria, and Iberis create compositional unity. At the base of the greenwall is a sandbox: another nest within which children play. Because the greenwall is located above the children's sandbox, special care was taken to choose non-toxic plants, in addition to edibles such as basil, rosemary, sage and thyme, and strawberries.

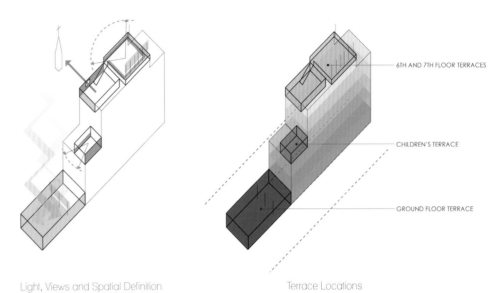

Light, Views and Spatial Definition

6TH AND 7TH FLOOR TERRACES

CHILDREN'S TERRACE

GROUND FLOOR TERRACE

Terrace Locations

TIPS

Microclimate
The local climatic conditions in work or living places, mainly include four parameters of temperature, humidity, air velocity (wind speed) and thermal radiation conditions. It will directly affect one's mood, spirit, health, comfort and efficiency.

The teak screens continue along the roof terrace and bind the entire space, opening the views to the visually active surroundings. The church spire reappears here: the upper terrace is oriented towards the church, using it as a foreground of a larger, borrowed, urban landscape. River birch trees provide screening and afternoon shade along the terrace's western edge, and sun-loving meadow grasses and perennials work together to visually filter the urban context and reinforce a sense of enclosure. The contrast between the lush planting and refined teak nest enriches the sensory experience and the plantings provide a horticultural echo of the planting of nearby Central Park.

Song Sheng

COMMENT

The design of landscape explores all possibilities for its design and proposes that to translate the complex green structure into a single space. This project is simple and calm, it opens an life space for people to stay, think and feel, while conveys an idea of love life. When people appreciate the aesthetics, one can enjoy the benefits brought by the design, such as stormwater management, energy conservation, heat preservation and so on. The King wall of plants in the garden creates a visual communication bridge between the garden and surrounding environment. All things in the garden can meet diversified demands of users.

"Enjoy fashion and simple alone."

OR_Roof Terrace

Landscape Architect: Andy Sturgeon Landscape and Garden Design
Location: London, UK
Site Area: 70 m²
Photography: Andrew Oi

CLIMATIC CONDITIONS

London belongs to temperate marine climate, warm in winter and cool in summer with small temperature difference in a year. It rains throughout the year, and enjoys more rain in winters.

PLANTS

astelia, nandina, bamboo

EDITOR'S CHOICE

The rooftop garden appears simple and elegant for its waterscape and wooden platform. The flame on the water is a bright point of the garden that brings in a glimmer of Reiki .

The client wanted a bold, striking roof top garden that was also simple and elegant. The 2 bedroom apartment is on the 3rd floor with little shelter from the sun, wind or rain and is not overlooked from neighbouring buildings. The living area of the apartment leads directly onto the rooftop through large glass sliding doors and the garden is to be primarily used at night so lighting was essential. Due to the physical limitations the site could not be fundamentally altered and the load bearing capacity had to be carefully considered. Floating timber bench seating, table and chairs provide a separate dining area and a highly flexible space.

The raised hardwood deck area allows easier access to and from living room. A sail fabric canopy suspended from metal beams provides all-weather shelter.

The long black reflective brimming pool was constructed from acrylic on a lightweight metal box frame. The water is actually very shallow but the black acrylic trough creates an illusion of depth with mirror like reflections. A gas Flambeaux flame emerging from water gives a dramatic light effect and provides a heat source as well as a focal point. White Terrazzo cubes and fixed planters of architectural planting such as Astelia, Nandina and Bamboo provide evergreen screening.

TIPS

Water and Wood

When water features are set in a rooftop garden, waterproof and leaking must be noticed. The edge of a large water feature, such as a pool, can be molded by concrete curbs in various ways. No matter what method is chosen, the pour-in water should be as shallow to the same level of the edge of the pool. But if the inner wall of the pool is painted into black, the depth of water reaching 10~15 inches (25.4~38.1 cm) is enough to give people a impression of unfathomable.

Wooden platform is general needed to do some anticorrosive processing, the water or soil part should be coated with paint or asphalt oil, to prolong the service life. If use anticorrosive wood directly, it is better to choose non-toxic or low toxicity, to reduce to hazard to human body and environment.

COMMENT

The design maximizes visual scale for such a small place. Garden space designed as an open is space without covering facilities to enhance the sense of empty. The design attaches great importance on rational application of landscape materials and clever mix of colorful plants, which fully embodies the garden's fullness and beauty. In conditions of relative constraints on the roof, the use of sustainable technology give the whole space flexibility through the exquisite water feature design.

Song Sheng

"Romantic moments win all the bustling in life."

Chelsea Roof Garden

Landscape Architect: Jinny Blom Limited, Landscape Design
Location: London, UK
Site Area: 225 m²
Photography: Jinny Blom, Robert Straver

CLIMATIC CONDITIONS

London belongs to temperate marine climate, warm in winter and cool in summer with small temperature difference in a year. It rains throughout the year, especially in winters.

PLANTS

echium fastuosum, salvia candelabrum, myrtle, crocosmia"lucifer", euphorbia mellifera, perovskia, tamarix ramosissima, campsis radicans, genista aetnensis, convolvulus sabatius, cytisus battandieri, lupinus arboreus

EDITOR'S CHOICE

The design breaks through the traditional style of the original garden, sun-proof Eastern Mediterranean-type vegetation to, enrich the viewing experience. At the same time, the reflective pool effectively draws on the advantages and avoids the disadvantage of small space. It is a completely new roof garden with sea garden features.

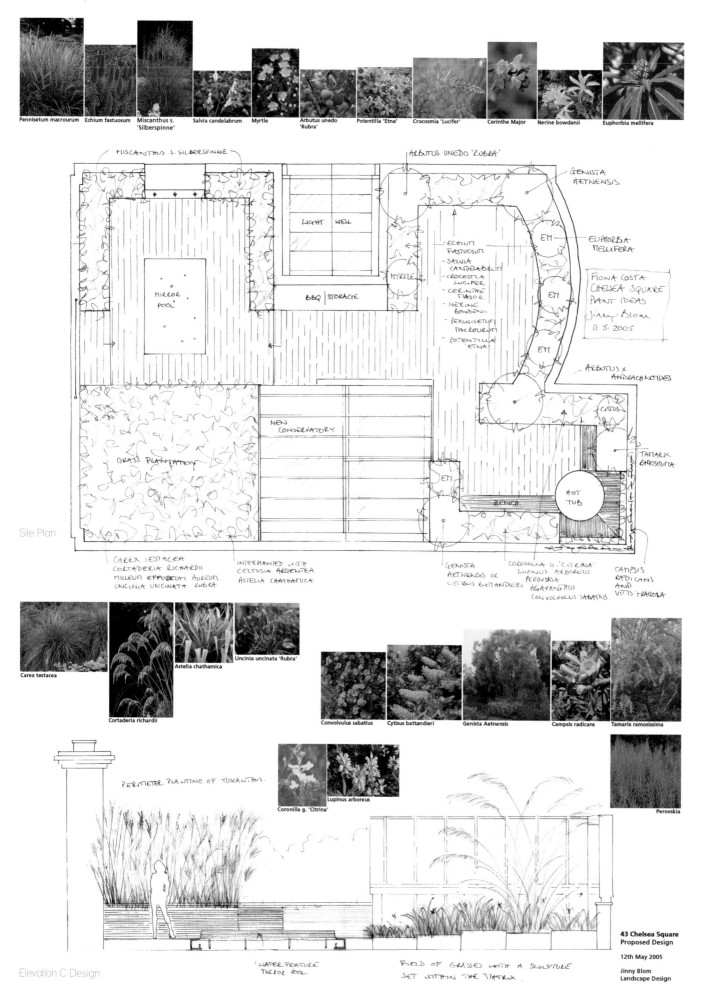

Pennisetum macrourum | Echium fastuosum | Miscanthus s. 'Silberspinne' | Salvia candelabrum | Myrtle | Arbutus unedo 'Rubra' | Potentilla 'Etna' | Crocosmia 'Lucifer' | Cerinthe Major | Nerine bowdenii | Euphorbia mellifera

MISCANTHUS S. SILBERSPINNE

ARBUTUS UNEDO 'RUBRA'

GENISTA AETNENSIS

LIGHT WELL

EUPHORBIA MELLIFERA

MYRTLE

MIRROR POOL

BBQ | STORAGE

ECHIUM FASTUOSUM
SALVIA CANDELABRUM
CROCOSMIA LUCIFER
CERINTHE MAJOR
NERINE BOWDENII
PENNISETUM MACROURUM
POTENTILLA 'ETNA'

FIONA COSTA
CHELSEA SQUARE
PLANT IDEAS
Jinny Blom
11. 5. 2005

ARBUTUS x ANDRACHNOIDES

CISTUS

NEW CONSERVATORY

TAMARIX RAMOSISSIMA

GRASS PLANTATION

BENCH

HOT TUB

Site Plan

CAREX TESTACEA
CORTADERIA RICHARDII
MILLEUM EFFUSUM AUREUM
UNCINIA UNCINATA RUBRA

INTERPLANTED WITH
CELTISIA ARGENTEA
ASTELIA CHATHAMICA

GENISTA
AETNENSIS OR
CYTISUS BATTANDIERI

CORONILLA G. 'CITRINA'
LUPINUS ARBOREUS
PEROVSKIA
AGAPANTHUS
CONVOLVULUS SABATIUS

CAMPSIS
RADICANS
AND
VITIS FRAGOLA

Carex testacea

Cortaderia richardii

Astelia chathamica

Uncinia uncinata 'Rubra'

Convolvulus sabatius | Cytisus battandieri | Genista Aetnensis | Campsis radicans | Tamarix ramosissima

PERIMETER PLANTING OF MISCANTHUS.

Coronilla g. 'Citrina'

Lupinus arboreus

Perovskia

43 Chelsea Square
Proposed Design

12th May 2005

Jinny Blom
Landscape Design

Elevation C Design

'WATER FEATURE
MIRROR POOL

FIELD OF GRASSES WITH A SCULPTURE
SET WITHIN THE TAMARIX.

It is rare in London, a city dominated by Victorian pitched roofs, to find a domestic house with a large flat roof. It was built in the 1920's and has the great advantage of a large flat roof, a rather nice copper clad dormer room that opens onto the roof and a good parapet wall around 1000 mm high. As well as this it has a dramatic chimney breast which makes a good feature.

With any roof garden design one has to start with the potential problem of weight. We discovered there was a substantial weak spot in the middle of the roof at the front and this assisted in designing a solution. Any roof has a slightly maritime feel and this garden was no exception. It is open to the great skies above and this exposure gives it a unique character.

Our client wanted a dining area, a 'chill out' area and a water feature. These easily fitted into the space. The garden is built of large planters clad in curved battens of hardwood- these are for safety as it makes it harder to reach the edge. We created a curved sun screen with a huge dining table below and many very good dinner parties have been held on the roof. The water feature is a mirror pool and is set over the weak spot in the roof so no one can stand on it.

The planting is mainly Mediterranean as it can cope with the
level of exposure. It is rich, flowery and beautiful all year round.

TIPS

Reduce Loading
While in the perspective of loading reduction, it needs to reduce the weight of landscape structure according to roof structure, and on the other hand, to reduce the weight of roofing materials, including transform the gravel drainage layer into light-weight materials and so on.

Pang Wei

COMMENT

This project creates a small relax garden in the tight space. Luxuriant flowers and trees, not only good for the body, but also for the health and mood.

"Waste into treasure, a garden of colors and poetry."

Unfolding Terrace

Landscape Architect: Terrain-NYC, Inc.
Location: New York, USA
Photography: Terrain-NYC, Inc., Andrea Brizzi

CLIMATIC CONDITIONS

New York has a relatively mild climate with four distinct seasons, but in the conversion of the seasons, there will be high and low-temperature changes. Summers often reach temperatures above 30℃ , while winters will drop below 0℃ and often snow.

PLANTS

sedum, grasses, rudbeckia, fernery, birches

EDITOR'S CHOICE

The wood platform around the terrace create a level sense in the plane and a continuous space. A poetry wall set off vertical stratification of drought-tolerant native plants as the background, making e the all space in a deep poetic atmosphere.

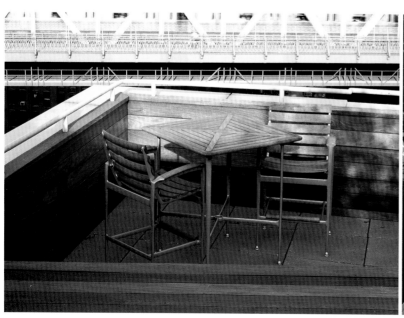

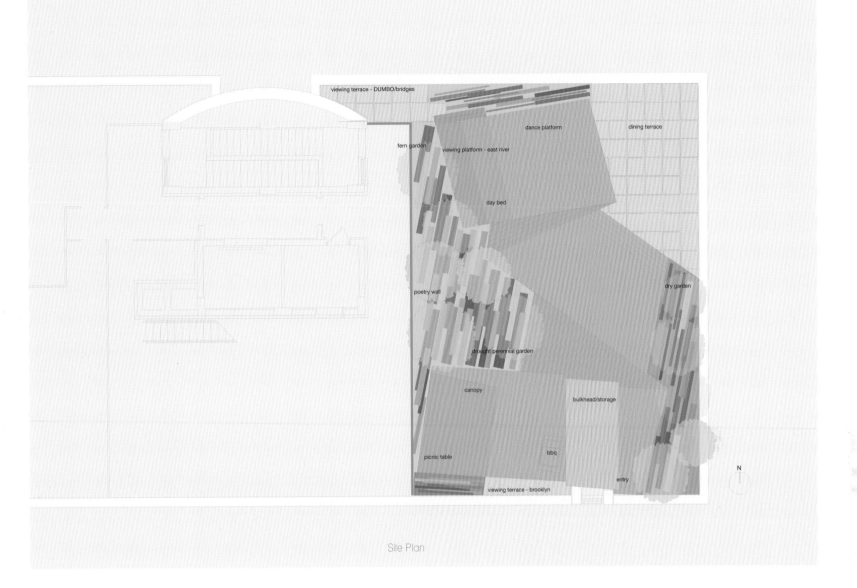

viewing terrace - DUMBO/bridges

dance platform

dining terrace

fern garden

viewing platform - east river

day bed

dry garden

poetry wall

drought perennial garden

canopy

bulkhead/storage

picnic table

bbq

entry

viewing terrace - brooklyn

N

Site Plan

The deck is conceived as a continuous surface that folds up and around the terrace, constructing programmed space for client's myriad programmatic needs for dance space, dining area, viewing platform with daybed, lounging and garden. The deck creates space and breaks it down, creating a fluid experience while containing the program of the site. At the same time, the folded structure masks vents and bulkheads on the roof space and provides storage, creating opportunities from design challenges. Each level of the site is marked with an illuminated resin panel, emphasizing the level changes and the underlying structure of the site – the varied but continuous surfaces.

As a larger strategy of urban green roofs, the Unfolding Terrace contributes to the urban ecology by reclaiming a previously barren space for both human occupation and wildlife, contributing to habitat and biodiversity. A sunny site, the roofscape is planted with drought tolerant species, including a palette of native plantings, sedum, grasses and rudbeckia. Groves of native river birch enhance the abstracted pattern on the poetry wall. In a shaded area a fernery adds diversity. As a roof deck, this project was constructed entirely on structure. An irrigation system tailored for low-water use plants was installed. On structure, there was not much room for soil depth. The birches are planted in a large, low (18") depth planter, so that the roots will form a shallow mat, which helps stabilize the entire grove, with each of the trees interacting to form an ecological system.

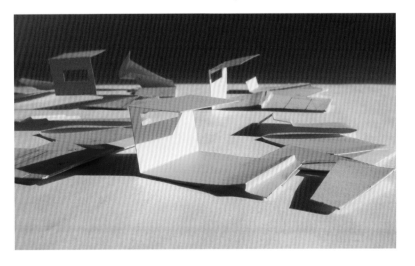

An urban roofscape that celebrates the spectacle of the city, the Unfolding Terrace negotiates the scale of the city's industrial landscape of infrastructure with the atmosphere of the garden living space. The decked surface folds across the roof, organizing program by creating constructed volumes of space. With a site specific commissioned poetry wall, the roofscape points to a new idea of nature in the city mediated by culture and artistic interpretation.

The space embodies a performance based understanding of landscape with the various elements performing functions that enhance the experience of the space. A poetry wall, constructed out of billboard sign materials, connects the space to the surrounding Dumbo roofscape including nearby billboards, shifting the scales of experiences of the city from the larger urban landscape, to the intimate roofspace, and back out again into urban experience. An East Village poet was commissioned to write a poem specific to the place.

The buildings meet the mountains, and thus horizon - where water towers, still as mountains, green the heart of urbankind - offer respite to birdkind, with its equanimous eye of flight as jets glide by the three sisters. bridges - as scents of commerce and blossom blend - as stars begin the dark with light - change thrives in skylines and hours, louder near rivers of traffic and bridges - bridges that star the sky with cables and arches - unmoved by change as they mother the city - almost as constant as the elements themselves—the bridge is daughter to tide.

The lighting design of the space extends the life of the terrace, activating the space at night and transforming the landscape into nocturnal spectacle. The level changes in the decking glow with a wash of light from illuminated resin panels. The edge plantings are enlivened, drawing attention to the edges, while attention is drawn away from the people on the deck, who remain darkened and therefore retain their privacy.

TIPS

Poetry and landscape design
Landscape is a pluralistic art, its spirit linked with poetry, literature, art inextricably. The combination of landscape and poetry is a pursuit of the aesthetic artistic conception, and is also an ideal state that designers take efforts to get.

COMMENT

Originally straightforward platform becomes rich just because of folding, and the poetry wall behind dancing plants were impressed by people on this garden.

Pang Wei

"Serenity and style above the Village."

Greenwich Penthouse

Landscape Architect: Dirtworks Landscape Architecture, PC
Location: New York, USA
Site Area: 131 m²
Photography: Andrew Bordwin, Dirtworks Landscape Architecture, PC

CLIMATIC CONDITIONS

New York has a relatively mild climate with four distinct seasons, but in the changing of the seasons, there will be high and low temperatures changes. Summers often reach temperatures above 30 ℃ , while winters will drop below 0 ℃ and often snow.

PLANTS

Trees- Pinus heldreichii, Bosnian Pine, Amelanchier Grandiflora, Pinus mugho, Shrubs-Ilex verticillata 'Sparkleberry', Ilex verticillata 'Jim Dandy', Perennials-Pennisetum alopecuroides, Gultheria procumbens, Amsonia hubrichtii, Hedera helix, Vinca minor, Sempervivum

EDITOR'S CHOICE

The terrace garden is an extension of a renovated penthouse in New York's Greenwich Village and boasts sweeping views across the Village and city skyline. There is a sense of serenity and calmness within the garden as a reprieve from the hustle of high-density urban living. The garden offers a variety of distinct settings with minimal maintenance. The plant palette consists of native grasses, trees and shrubs. Low maintaince plants were carefully selected for their local hardiness and visual interest throughout the year. They offer a haven for local and migrant birds. Simple materials and a direct planning strategy help extend the elegant style and refined character of the interior spaces to the outdoors. The terrace garden design is timeless and ultimately reflects the clients' sensibilities.

There is a trust and collaboration between the landscape architect and these long-time clients, which provide the opportunity to shape the context of their everyday lives. Design and construction took place with minimal drawings. The result is inviting and tranquil garden.

The design, materials and construction had to be practical and appropriate. Cedar pallets, chosen to minimize heat and glare, define and connect sitting and dining spaces. The pallet geometry contrasts with gentle curved planters and native plants, which enclose spaces, and frame classic city views. The cedar pallet deck completes the setting and invites one to relax and enjoy the outdoors, which becomes an extension of the penthouse itself.

TIPS

Rooftop gardens offer exposure to the elements and views of the surrounding neighbors. In order to minimize unnecessary exposure and creative a private space for relaxation, consider using plant materials to create visual distinction. One can screen neighbors views by selecting small trees or thick shrubs that obstruct direct line sight whether one is sitting or standing. Plants should be somewhat resistant to harsh rain, wind and cold as they may be more exposed to these elements. Wind screens or selection of plants that tolerate this buffeting may be essential.

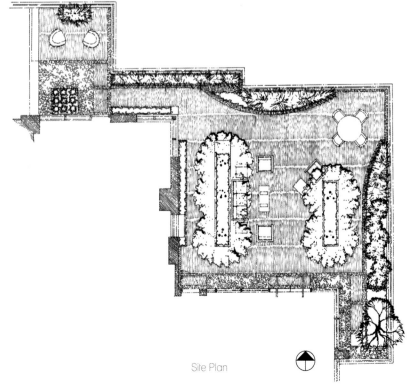

Site Plan

The exterior spaces are framed by a series of custom planters cantilevered over a perimeter bed of rounded stones. There is a natural blend of wood, planters and pebbles which balance the ambiance and invite one to linger. The garden is filled with grasses of varying heights and textures, and the quiet rustling grass in the wind forms an effective barrier to the traffic below. The small native trees frame a seating area and offers shade from the sun. A corner of the garden contains a small seating area. The garden mediates between the interior of the apartment and the city. In front of the window, a low table displaying pots of seasonal color forms a dramatic foreground to midtown views from the study to the dining room beyond.

The planting plan highlights seasonal changes and frames city views from interior spaces. Sweeps of native grasses and shrubs frame views of a nearby water tower. An ivy-covered steel trellis and small flowering trees enhances midtown skyline views.

Reducing the heat island effect of the rooftop was considered essential. The design uses lightweight, eco-friendly renewable materials, and a simple palette of native plants that thrives with an integrated pest management and a drip irrigation system.

David Kamp

COMMENT

In order to minimize unnecessary exposure and creative a private space for relaxation, consider using plant materials to create visual distinction. One can screen neighbors' views by selecting small trees or thick shrubs that obstruct direct line sight whether one is sitting or standing. Plants should be somewhat resistant to harsh rain, wind and cold as they may be more exposed to these elements. Wind screens or selection of plants that tolerate this buffeting may be essential.

"Where nature meets fashion"

Manhattan Roof Terrace

Landscape Architect: Sawyer/Berson Architecture & Landscape Architecture, LLP
Location: New York, USA
Site Area: 132.67 m²
Photography: Sawyer/Berson, Bill Cunningham, Dana Gallagher

CLIMATIC CONDITIONS

New York is in temperate continental climate with warm summers and cool winters that leads to a temperature difference in a year. It has concentrated rainfalls in certain periods and four distinct seasons.

PLANTS

vine

EDITOR'S CHOICE

The renovated project shows the layout of modernism. The furniture is simple, clean and peace with growing plants forms a strong contrast between static to live .

To create the setting for this 1,428 square foot roof terrace, an existing postmodern roof pavilion was demolished to make way for a modern architectural framework inspired by the works of American architect Paul Rudolph, and French architects Jean Prouvé and Pierre Chareau. A steel-framed platform was installed, onto which a program of garden elements were placed: a fountain, pergola and planters, as well as an outdoor kitchen and shower.

The custom cast concrete pavers, sandblasted glass panels, painted steel framework, and perforated stainless steel panels contrast with the lush plantings chosen for their color, texture, scent as well as hardiness to the extreme conditions of New York City roof tops.

The terrace features include the lounge area, formal dining area covered by a pergola, granite and glass mosaic fountain, outdoor cooking and bar area, and an outdoor shower. Other elements include a site audio system, extensive lighting, and an electronic drip irrigation system. Also, six built-in infrared heaters were installed within the pergola structure to extend the outdoor dining season.

Terrace Plan

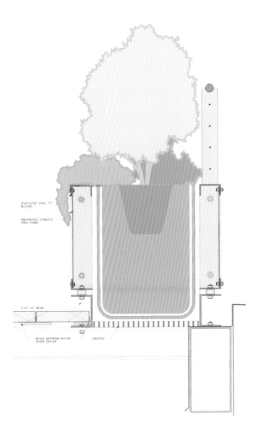

Typical Planter Section

East West Section Looking North

East West Section Looking South

As a requirement by the building management company, the entire roof terrace improvement was designed to be disassembled and removed. The structural steel frame that supports the terrace paving, pergola, fountain, planters, and railing is anchored to four structural columns of the building.

Structural steel support framework for the paving system; custom concrete pavers; perforated stainless steel panels and painted steel framing for all the planters throughout the terrace, and the cabinets at the outdoor cooking and bar area; painted steel and stainless steel railings; perforated stainless steel wall system surrounding the outdoor shower; black honed granite for the bar, dining table top and fountain exterior; and, non iridescent black glass mosaic tile for the fountain. The pots are custom fabricated color integrated cast stone, and all furnishings are also custom fabrications.

TIPS

Effective Maintenance

It is the key to ensure a healthy and beautiful roof garden. Most plants on roof gardens are planted in containers; without natural foundation to provide water, drainage, evaporation, consumption may result in water and nutrient depletion and finally cause death of plants. Therefore, periodic maintenance is necessary to supply lost and absorbed water and nutrients for plants; attentions should also pay to their growth situations to ensure they do not grow over the edge of containers.

COMMENT

Kitchen, dining room, bathroom, living room in outdoor garden based on the modern technologies seems romantic and bold, the garden seems to by "slavery romantic" as in the Chinese ancient garden.

Pang Wei

"All the towers, only love here."

684 BROADWAY

Landscape Architect: Balmori Associates
Client: Matthew A Blesso, Blesso Properties
Location: New York, USA
Site Area: 204.4 m²
Photography: Mark Dye

CLIMATIC CONDITIONS

New York has a relatively mild climate with four distinct seasons, but in the conversion of the seasons, there will be high and low-temperature changes. Summers often reach temperatures above 30℃, while winters will drop below 0℃ and often snow.

PLANTS

Elephant Ears, black bamboo, euonymus

EDITOR'S CHOICE

The project creates a seamless and natural transition space through the creation of space reconstruction and a new connection, showing the rich diversity of vegetation. It reflects the designer's original intent, that is, the harmony between architecture and nature, and magnification of biodiversity.

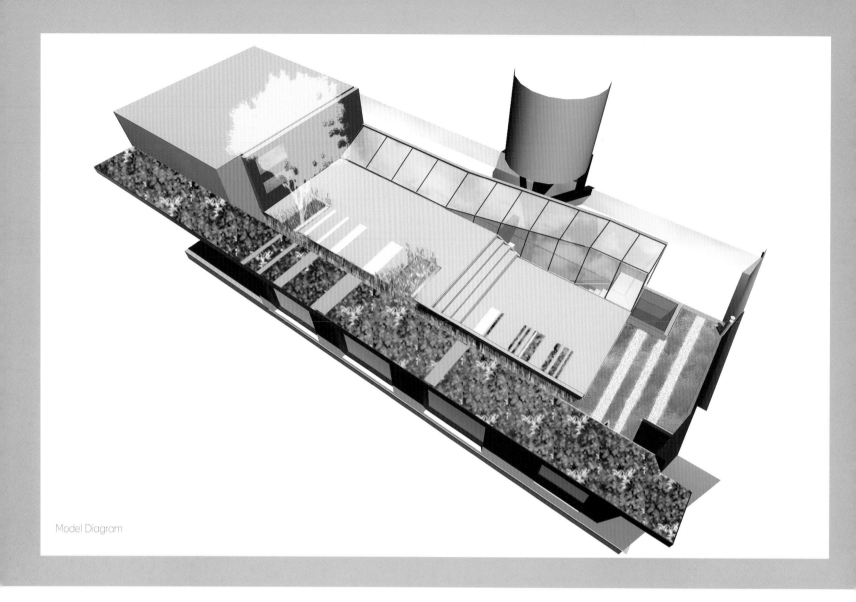

Model Diagram

The project at 684 Broadway is an effort to explore the interface of the built and natural environment. Reconfiguring the space in between and making new connections creates more fluid passages; not blurring the line between landscape and architecture, but widening it. This thick interface creates the opportunity for new types of spaces. Alternating sheaves of landscape and building on both horizontal and vertical planes create transitions within this widened line.

This interface becomes a sustainable strategy that aims to maximize biodi¬versity and sustainable design in this urban site by extending green space both horizontally and vertically within the renovated apartment and exterior roof space. The result, hypernature, is an artificial spectacle of constructed nature. Natural forms and phenomena are revealed and re-visioned into a magical landscape for living. Ecology and art meet at the surface creating an explosion of life within the urban context.

TIPS

Biodiversity
Biodiversity provides many important environmental services, such as maintaining the topsoil, maintaining water catchments, providing pollination by insects, bringing useful birds and other living beings, and deciding regional climate etc.

Suspended above the sea of grasses is a bi-level ipe deck. On the lower level a small gravel path leads to a look out pod with views over the lower east side, an outdoor shower and on the opposite side of the stair bulkhead, a more pri¬vate enclave with jacuzzi and sunning deck. Five steps lead to the upper level with an outdoor kitchen and grill lounging space. Opposite the parapet, the bulkhead rises into the sky. Densely planted with stepable plants one can lie on the slope and watch cloud rushing overhead. A staircase leads to the top from which there is a 360 °C view of the Lower East side.

The interface begins with an interior garden beneath a twenty-foot long sky-light. Filled with large leaved Elephant Ears and black bamboo, the plants create an ascending green carpet beneath the floating stairs to the roof. Above the delicate bamboo fronds, through a glass partition separating the garden from master bathroom, a green wall planted with euonymus is visible. This improbable swath of vertical vegetation climbs the wall colliding with a second skylight through which is visible of the rooftop planting.

Pang Wei

COMMENT

The slope design is impressive. But the design is not limited on the surface, the whole garden has the function of rainwater collection... It gives us some inspirations: Visual impacts are important, but not the only key element.

"It is a perfect place for rare moments to be on your own."

Rooftop Terrace and Kitchen Garden

Landscape Architect: Merilen Mentaal - MentaalLandscapes
Client: Merilen Mentaal
Location: Tallinn, Estonia
Site Area: 45 m² (rooftop terrace), 15 m² (kitchen garden)
Cost: $ 4,000~5,000
Photography: Merilen Mentaal

CLIMATIC CONDITIONS

Tallinn has cold and wet winters (down to -25° C) and cool summers (up to 28° C) with prevailing western winds.

PLANTS

Hamamelis x intermedia 'Jelena', Philadelphus 'Belle Etoile', Abies koreana 'Schneestern', Salvia nemorosa 'Caradonna', Malva moschata 'Alba', Nepeta faassenii 'Walker's Low', various Echinacea purpurea and tulipa

EDITOR'S CHOICE

The designer uses a bold design to create an unique and beautiful garden for herself! By cleverly dividing the small area on the roof, a small world both for leisure and party is born.

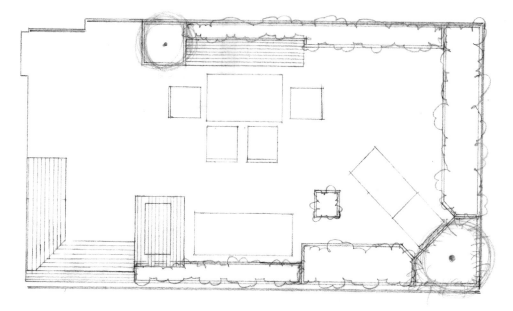

Terrace Sketch

These suburban terrace gardens situate in a residential neighbourhood, very close to the sea enjoying the fresh air but suffering from frequent harsh winds. Ontop of an apartment building, the 5m x 9 m rooftop garden is built for maximizing the outdoor living, dining and evening BBQ-s, sunbathing and endless gardening activities as it is designer's own garden, therefore a perfect place for trying out different plants and new combinations.

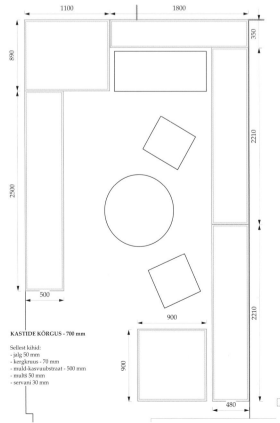

KASTIDE KÕRGUS - 700 mm

Sellest kihid:
- jalg 50 mm
- kergkruus - 70 mm
- muld-kasvuubstraat - 500 mm
- multš 50 mm
- servani 30 mm

Dimensions for built-in planters

Raised planters are made of 50mm x 50 mm pinewood material, lined by pond-liner inside and filled with lighter substrate mixed with good garden soil.

Seating area has a built-in bench backed by narrow planter with grasses, mimicing the natural grassy seaside. Another built-in L-shape seating area allows for additional lounging and larger crowd to be entertained.

Further out and partly screened by dark grey container with highly scented English roses 'Munstead Wood' is the loungechair area, facing the daytime sun and surrounded by lush aromatic planting. Many smaller containers and little details like mirrors, metal shelves with annual and perennial plants add to the slightly wild and natural atmosphere of the terrace.

Kitchen terrace is on a lower level, built above a walkway from entrance to the yard. Covered by roof but open on both sides, it offers a very challenging garden area which is mostly shady and quite often windy but a lovely spacious and green addition to the small glass-walled kitchen. One side of the garden has climbers trained on metal wires and cool, shade-loving green planting, including hostas and different mints. The sunny side offers everything edible – strawberries, arctic brambles and many herbs – lemon balm, thyme, chives, rosemary, basil, parsley, catmint etc.

Equally important are many berries and vegetables grown separately or mixed with perennials – raspberries, strawberries, cherry tomatoes, rocket, blackberries, chillies and chard.

PUIT - 50 x 50 mm, vahedega 20-30 mm; Viimistlus sama mis alumisel terrassil
MULD - segu mustast mullast ja 0-turbast; 8,1 m2 pinda
KASTI SISU - Jalg 50 mm; perforeeritud põhi; kergkruus 50 mm; mulla-turbasegu; peene fraktsiooniga multš 50 mm, servast 30 mm allpool;
    Kasti küljed kaetud tiigikilega

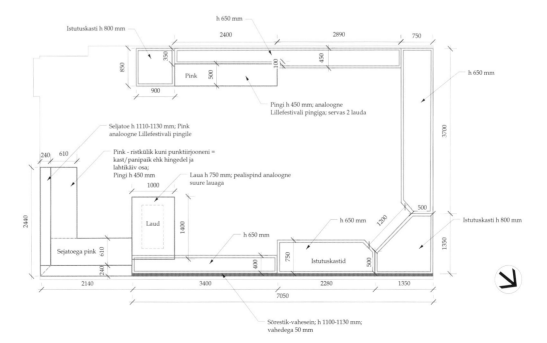

Istutuskasti h 800 mm

h 650 mm

2400   2890   750

850 350 100 450

Pink 500

900

h 650 mm

Pingi h 450 mm; analoogne
Lillefestivali pingiga; servas 2 lauda

3700

Seljatoe h 1110-1130 mm; Pink
analoogne Lillefestivali pingile

Pink - ristkülik kuni punktiirjooneni =
kast/panipaik ehk hingedel ja
lahtikäiv osa;
Pingi h 450 mm

Laua h 750 mm; pealispind analoogne
suure lauaga

240 610

1000

2440

Laud

1400

610

500

h 650 mm

1200

Istutuskasti h 800 mm

Sejatoega pink

240

h 650 mm

750

h 650 mm

1350

400

Istutuskastid

500

2140   3400   2280   1350

7050

Sörestik-vahesein; h 1100-1130 mm;
vahedega 50 mm

Dimensions and Material Specifications for the rooftop garden

TIPS

Before planting in rooftop gardens, designers need to do deep research about local wind-resistant plants and choose plants that withstand these conditions. Large leaves should be avoided as strong winds rip the leaves. Meanwhile, attention should also be paid to light-weight facilities to avoid causing damages.

Song Sheng

COMMENT

Both in the choice of materials and the design of space structure, designers use every inch of roof well. Bold plant disposition and the textures of spatial materials form a good echo effect. In tight place, the height of plants and landscape elements are used clearly to create a practical activity place in the limited space. There is also roof pool along the edge of platform, creating a feeling of inclusiveness and enclosure. People can feel the social space and private space at the same time, watching times fly, or entertaining friends and family.

ECOLOGICAL
GREEN

"The overflowing greenery is a summons for happiness."

Giant Interactive Group Campus

Landscape Architect: SWA Group
Client: Giant Investment Co., Ltd
Location: Shanghai, China
Site Area: 182,109 m^2
Roof Area: 15,222 m^2
Photography: Tom Fox, Principal, SWA Group; Iwan Baan

CLIMATIC CONDITIONS

Shanghai features the subtropical monsoon climate. The annual average temperature is 22.4°C, and annual rainfall is more than 2,100 mm. July-September each year as the rainy season, precipitation occupy two-fifths of year.

PLANTS

mature camphors, sweet olives, Liriope palatyphylla, Carex oshimensis 'Evergold', Sedum spectabile 'Boreau', Stachys lanata, Vinca major 'Variegata', Oenothera speciosa, Tradescantia reflexa 'Rafin', Spirea x bumalda 'Golden Mound', Ajuga multiflora 'Bunge', Herba sedi sarmentosi, Chinese Sedum, lantana

EDITOR'S CHOICE

The design with green building technology provides open space for employees in their leisure time and overcomes the workplace situation with career officers sitting in front of the computer, surrounded by inanimate objects. The ingenious roof structure mitigates the extreme slope conditions, allows reasonable soil control and promotes the natural growth of vegetation.

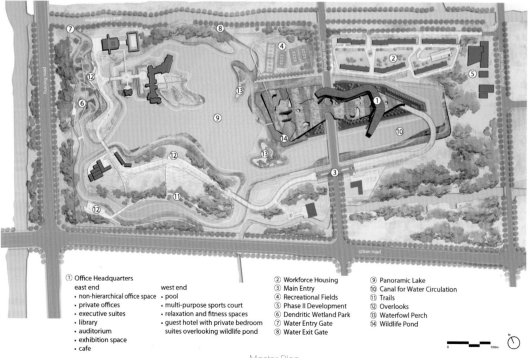

① Office Headquarters
east end
· non-hierarchical office space
· private offices
· executive suites
· library
· auditorium
· exhibition space
· cafe

west end
· pool
· multi-purpose sports court
· relaxation and fitness spaces
· guest hotel with private bedroom
  suites overlooking wildlife pond

② Workforce Housing
③ Main Entry
④ Recreational Fields
⑤ Phase II Development
⑥ Dendritic Wetland Park
⑦ Water Entry Gate
⑧ Water Exit Gate

⑨ Panoramic Lake
⑩ Canal for Water Circulation
⑪ Trails
⑫ Overlooks
⑬ Waterfowl Perch
⑭ Wildlife Pond

Master Plan

This project demonstrates the success of native and adaptive plants thriving on extreme conditions, habitat creation, green building technology and employee access to recreational open space.

All too often, the workplace is where most employees spend their time, sitting in front of the computer screen surrounded by inanimate objects. This lack of visual and physical stimulation can cause stress and depression for those who do not find an escape from work. The challenge lies in creating an environment that can provide this respite while functioning as a robust living organism. Wandering through the campus, the employees may experience a surge of fragrance coming from the Sweet Olives while watching birds in search of prey. Other amenities for active recreation such as outdoor multi-purpose sports court, indoor pool, and additional relaxation and fitness spaces further provide alternative means to stimulate, relax, and refresh one's physical and mental acuity.

Strategic placement of landforms within the manmade lake provided nesting grounds for waterfowls, protecting them from potential predators. The site was formerly a tree farm with mono-cultural stands of mature Camphors (Cinnamomum camphora) and Sweet Olives (Osmanthus fragrans). 90% of the existing trees are salvaged, relocated to various parts of the site, and amended with a variety of other tree species to promote biodiversity richness and seasonal interests.

Surrounded by waterways is the headquarters building for Giant Interactive Group. An expansive green roof of 15,222 square meters envelopes the structure, blurring the edges where landscape and building meet. The green roof was designed to be a low maintenance "meadow" that requires little watering and naturalizes over time. Unlike a typical green roof, the surfaces fold, soar and dip. The undulating roof structure plunges into the ground plane at points, dipping into the wildlife pond and coming into contact with the pedestrian plaza.

TIPS

Thickness of Soil
Soil thickness of the roof garden is controlled to the minimum. The soil thickness of cultivation depends on the permit loading of a load-bearing floor, taking into account the bulk density of the materials used and the planting maintenance situation. The thickness of the soil layer for lawn to be walked on is 20-25 cm; soil thickness for shrubs is 40-50 cm; arbor soil thickness is 110 cm.

The extreme slope conditions, some run as steep as 53 °C, pose significant challenges for vegetation. An innovative system of reinforced concrete cleats, spanned by steel angles and gabions, are laid parallel to each sloping surface. The system functions as large self contained cells holding the soil in place and thus minimizing slumping and erosion due to gravity.

Planting Analysis

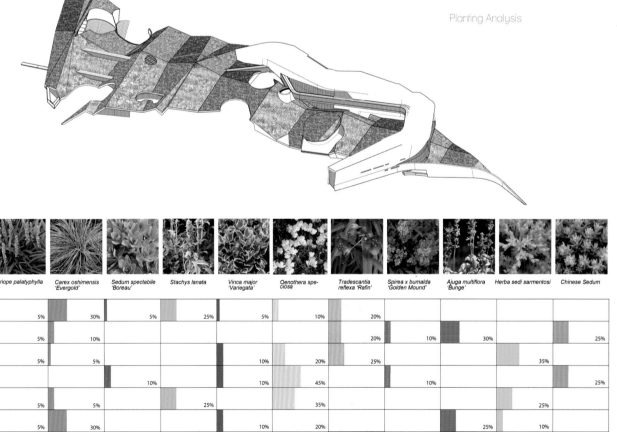

	Liriope palatyphylla	*Carex oshimensis 'Evergold'*	*Sedum spectabile 'Boreau'*	*Stachys lanata*	*Vinca major 'Variegata'*	*Oenothera speciosa*	*Tradescantia reflexa 'Rafin'*	*Spirea x bumalda 'Golden Mound'*	*Ajuga multiflora 'Bunge'*	*Herba sedi sarmentosi*	*Chinese Sedum*
Group 1- Ridge	5%	30%	5%	25%	5%	10%	20%				
Group 2- Valley	5%	10%					20%	10%	30%		25%
Group 3- NE	5%	5%			10%	20%	25%			35%	
Group 4- NW			10%		10%	45%		10%			25%
Group 5- SE	5%	5%		25%		35%				25%	
Group 6- SW	5%	30%			10%	20%			25%	10%	
Regular Water											
Moderate Water											
Sun											
Shade											

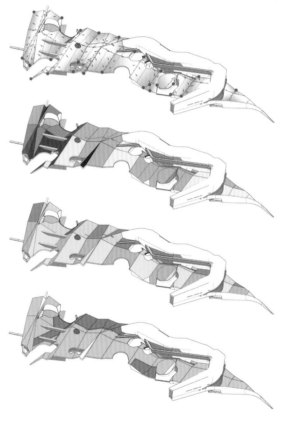

Landscape Systems

After a year-long testing and adjustments to plant species and mix percentages, eleven species were chosen based on the plant's native origin (seven species are native to China), plant rigor, ability to tolerate sun and shade, plant hardiness to dry soil and standing water, and seasonal flowering regimes. After only one season's growth, a pleasant surprise has been observed--the roofscape has become a haven for butterflies, particularly the Small Cabbage White butterfly (Pieris rapae).

EXTENSIVE GREEN ROOF SYSTEM

A. LIGHTWEIGHT PLANTING SOIL MIX

Ten inches of soil is laid to provide a substrate for plant roots to grow into as they become established.

B. FILTER FABRIC

This polypropylene fabric filter helps contain the soil and keep it from washing away, while also acting as a barrier between the planted surface and the building insulation.

C. STAINLESS STEEL GABION BASKETS

Filled with stone rip rap, the gabions provide structural support and aid in drainage.

D. DRAINAGE BOARD

Made of strong lightweight plastic, the trays help in the regulation and drainage of rain/irrigation water that percolates through the soil and fabric filter.

E. INSULATION

The insulation works with the vegetation to keep the building interior roughly ten degrees cooler than a standard roof. It also lowers the noise frequency by forty decibels.

F. ROOT BARRIER

Made of polyethylene, this barrier decreases the potential of roots penetrating the concrete structural slab by directing their growth away from the structure of the roof.

G. WATERPROOF MEMBRANE

This thin sheet composed of rubberized asphalt separates water and drainage runoff from the insulation layer away from the structure of the roof.

H. CONCRETE CLEAT

Reinforced concrete cleats are strategically placed along the roof structure to prevent soil movement across steeply sloped surfaces.

I. STEEL ANGLE

Steel bars attached to reinforced concrete blocks create a framework to stabilize the soil of steep sloping areas of the roof.

J. STRUCTURAL SLAB

The structural form work which makes up the buildings mounded roof.

Zhang Wenying

COMMENT

The project breaks the strict boundary between architecture and landscape, integrating them as a whole part. The green roof covered an area of 15 000 m² has offered solutions for earthing, soil consolidation, water preservation and drainage. Suitable plants are chosen after rigorous screened and mixed in different species; they need little maintenance and will form a natural community gradually with colorful flowers throughout the year so that the roof contributes to a nice working environment full of rustic charm and seasonal changes. The kind of architecture combining technology, art and ecology will become a future trend.

"Give roof a change — environmental reformation begins in small places."

Green Facelift for Sha Tin Sewage Treatment Works

Landscape Architect: Hong Kong Drainage Services Department, HKSAR Government
Location: Hong Kong, China
Green Roof Area: 3 000 m²
Cost: HK $ 2.6M

CLIMATIC CONDITIONS

Climatic Conditions: Hong Kong belongs to the subtropical monsoon climate, the annual average temperature is 22.4 °C, annual rainfall is more than 2,100 mm. July-September each year is the rainy season, precipitation occupying two-fifths of year.

EDITOR'S CHOICE

This project is the largest retrofitted green roof in Hong Kong with the features of low nursing, shallow-rooted, pest-resistant, wind-resistant, drought-tolerant and sunlight acceptable local plants. It offers an ecological continuity between the sewage treatment and the surrounding environment, which will be a model of modern factory building.

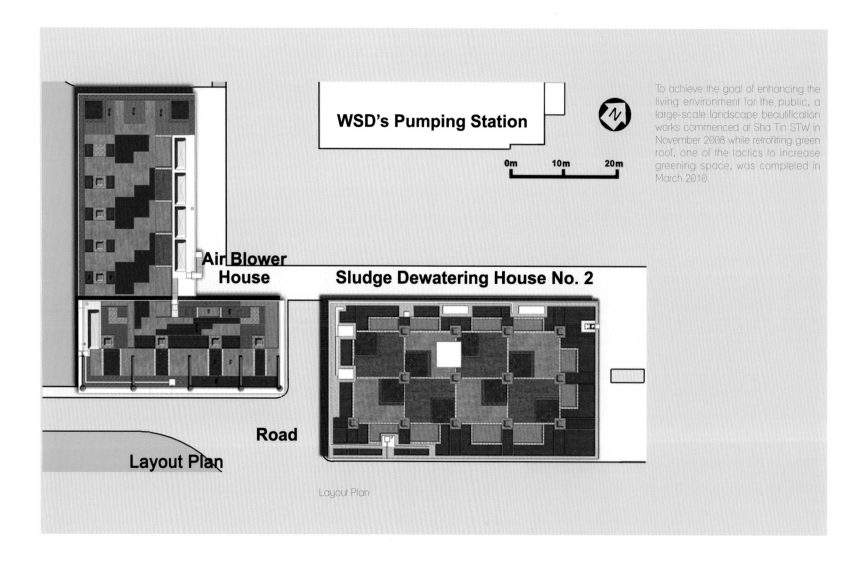

WSD's Pumping Station

To achieve the goal of enhancing the living environment for the public, a large-scale landscape beautification works commenced at Sha Tin STW in November 2008 while retrofitting green roof, one of the tactics to increase greening space, was completed in March 2010.

0m 10m 20m

Air Blower House

Sludge Dewatering House No. 2

Road

Layout Plan

Layout Plan

The design concept of the green roof is to use different colours of groundcovers to integrate with the existing Electrical & Mechanical facilities and pipeworks on roof, while providing proper maintenance access, to create a colourful design. The completed green roofs have tied in with the landscape beautification works of Sha Tin STW and visually extend the greening space to the Shing Mun River Channel.

To enhance the aesthetic values of the surrounding environment, four buildings in the STW next to Tate's Cairn Highway, which are visually sensitive to nearby residents, are selected to install about 3,000m² of retrofitted green roofs planted with 120,000 groundcovers in 11 different species and colours. Among the completed roofs, the one that covers an area of more than a standard swimming pool is currently the largest retrofitted green roof in Hong Kong.

TIPS

Ground covers refer to certain perennial herb, bushes and lianas with dense foliage and short bodies laid in a large area of bare ground or slopes or grown in damp and dark undergrowth or similar environment. Lawns, creeping foliage plants and perennial plants are familiar ground covers.

As the roof structure only allows 120mm thick soil depth for the retrofitted green roof, groundcover species that require low maintenance, with shallow root system, and are pest resistant, drought tolerant, resistant to wind and direct sunlight are selected.

Green roofs not only help to improve air quality but also reduce heat island effect. Besides, according to the findings of our previous research, green roofs can reduce indoor temperature 1.5 - 2.3°C, contributing in energy saving.

Green roofs improve the aesthetic value while the plants grown also bring the concrete roofs to life, making it become an ideal habitat for birds and insects. By providing guided tours to the local district councilors and residents, we can strengthen our relations with the community and solicit their valuable opinions on the greening works.

Site Plan

Angie AU YEUNG

COMMENT

This project is indeed a successful example showing how quality landscape works contribute significantly to infrastructure works. Through extensive planting, Sha Tin Sewage Treatment Works has become a new oasis in the district.

"Crush the seasonal green field into the soil fragrance."

Roof Garden Hotel St. Regis

Landscape Architect: KVR Arquitectura de Paisaje
Location: Mexico City, The United Mexican States
Site Area: 2, 000 m²
Photography: Eric Goethals, Kees Van Rooij

CLIMATIC CONDITIONS

Mexico City is located in the central highlands and basins of Mexico, surrounded by green hills. Due to its high altitude, it has cold winters and cool summers.

EDITOR'S CHOICE

Most plants to be chosen should have powerful insulate features, while adapt to harsh growing conditions, and the allocation of water resources with low consumption. As the extension facade of building, it covers the entire roof with the paving, under low costs of operation and maintenance, and shows out the ecological and social value of the project.

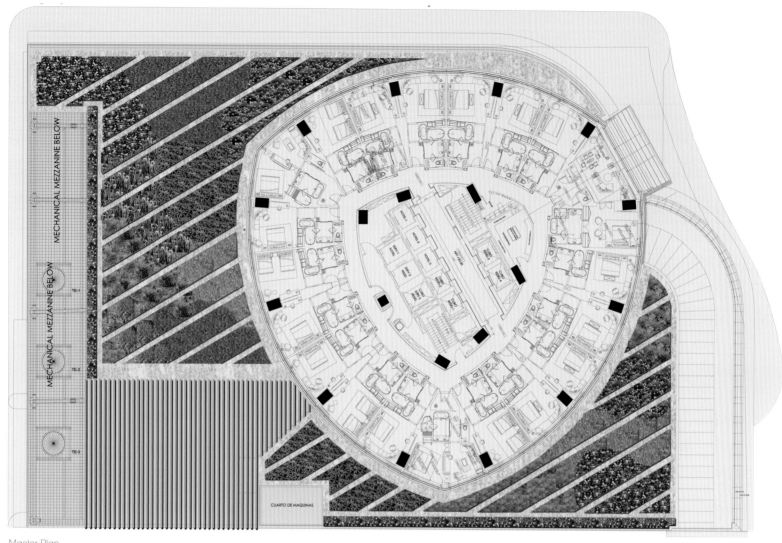

Master Plan

Model Diagram

TIPS

Garden Pavement

Through the changes of materials and patterns, garden pavement forms space edges and produces implications on people's minds to reach the effect of spatial segregation and functional changes. The paving have different colors, shapes, texture and forms, leading people to integrate into the landscape emotionally.

The project is executed on the roof garden above the basement on the fourth and fifth tower. The design consists of a series of parallel lines of roads and vegetation, referring as an eco of the façade of the building in its form and shape.

Design strategy for the landscape is to create unique and vigorous roof garden, both ecological and well equipped. Landscape design respects and lays emphasis on its natural resources and quality, including gallery, terrain, quality of drainage and storage, protection of vegetation growth environment. At the same time, upon sufficient consideration of relationship between landscape and architecture, and ensure the building quality and landscape stability, designer creates harmonious proportion space scale.

The landscape design started mainly from its chosen of plants and function, well-proportioned fields combined with the brief and fresh plants configuration to form a plane space with strong thorough feeling. It carries on a system to capture rainwater, the selection of the vegetation supports strong insulation and extreme conditions, plus it requires low consumption of water, this helps to have a low cost in maintenance, likewise, vegetation works as a thermal insulator, diminishing the use of air conditioning inside the building, making the building more sustainable.

It is a landscape combined ecological value and social value together as an organic whole, to create a piece of oasis for compact urban pattern, while increasing the region cultural ambience. It is accomplished a landscape from the next levels, and converts the roof of the basement in an extension of the building façade, under a low cost in operation and maintenance.

COMMENT

The plants layout on the rooftop garden fits well with the façade of the hotel, the texture of plants cultivation is almost the same with the façade's. Plants in different colors set in parallel lines form subtle curved changes; their vivid colors have softened the hardness of the building. In terms of function, the plants help to reduce indoor temperature, save resources and lower costs of hotel operations, featured the building in sustainable.

Zhang Wenying

The subtle essense of Japan permeates in these delicate rooftop gardens providing a new suprise with each view.

New Otani Hotel Roof Gardens

Landscape Architect: Keikan Sekkei Tokyo Co., Ltd.
Client: Nikken Sekkei, New Otani Hotel
Location: Chiyoda-ku, Tokyo Prefecture, Japan
Site Area: 2,500 m²

CLIMATIC CONDITIONS

Tokyo has a temperate maritime monsoon climate with four distinct seasons and abundant rainfall. Influenced by the East Asian Moonsoon summer brings heavy rains while winter is relatively dry with minimal snowfall.

PLANTS

Camellia hiemalis, Rhododendron indicum, Hibiscus syriacus, Indian Hawthorn, Liriope muscari 'Variegata', Lesser Periwinkle, Ophiopogon japonicas, Juniperus chinensis var. procumbens, Pinus pumila, Exochorda racemosa

EDITOR'S CHOICE

The bare roofs have been rebuilt into gardens decorated in Japanese elements. Different plants arranged in Japanese traditional modes exhibit the Janpanese modern style. The project has effectively reduced the heat island effect and storm water runoff in downtown Tokyo, forming an eco protection for the architecture.

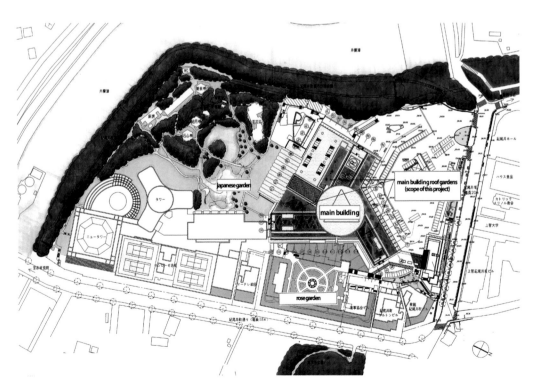

This project undertook the creation of roof gardens on the 17th floor roof (viewed from the restaurant) and the 3rd floor roof (top of the lower building), which were originally barren roofs, as part of the hotels renovations, necessary 40 years after the main building's construction. A unique spatial theme was developed defining the 17th floor roof as "Sky Garden" and the 3rd floor roof as "Relief Garden."

These roof gardens are designed to help reduce the heat-island phenomenon in the Tokyo metropolitan area, and reduce stormwater runoff. As such the Tokyo Metropolitan Government contributed financial aid to the project due to its environmental considerations under the "Cool Roof Promotion Project". When combined with the existing Japanese garden of the New Otani Hotel and the surrounding green areas, these new roof gardens contribute both to making the hotel property more attractive as well as making the urban area of Tokyo more beautiful. This project is recognized as not only a green roof but also a higher hospitality garden.

Overall Site Plan

TIPS

The Urban Heat Island Effect
It Refers to urban temperatures significantly higher than those of outlying suburbs.In recent years, the concentration of the urban population, industrial development, traffic congestion, serious air pollution, and buildings in the city mostly built of stone and concrete, has resulted in the urban annual average temperature being higher than the suburbs by about 2 ℃.

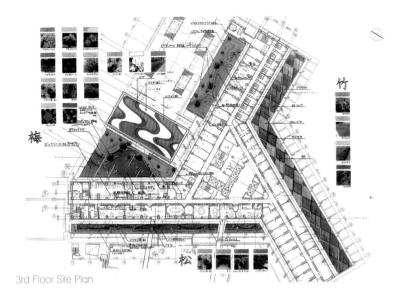

3rd Floor Site Plan

梅　竹　松

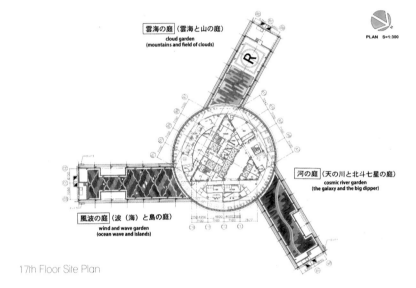

雲海の庭（雲海と山の庭）
cloud garden
(mountains and field of clouds)

河の庭（天の川と北斗七星の庭）
cosmic river garden
(the galaxy and the big dipper)

風波の庭（波（海）と島の庭）
wind and wave garden
(ocean wave and islands)

PLAN S=1:300

17th Floor Site Plan

Due to the projects location issues such as weight restrictions, and countermeasures against wind blow were carefully considered in the context of the existing building structure to achieve a higher quality garden. Custom designed lighting is prominently featured throughout the gardens, becoming focal points among the plant material, much of which is ground cover plantings. These custom lighting fixtures have developed a great reputation due to their traditional Japanese styling – modest yet a significant component of the overall landscape.

The theme for the 3rd floor roof garden is "Relief Garden", a space for guests to feel peace of mind as they view Japanese nature from their guest rooms. The gardens communicate the Japanese perception of nature expressed through "Ka-Cho-Fu-Getsu" (Flower, Bird, Wind, Moon), with each modern Japanese garden representing a different theme, "Pine", "Bamboo," and "Plum," each of which carries symbolic beauty for Japanese.

Owing to the 17th floor's fine vistas of the skyscrapers in the Shinjuku area, these gardens collectively are named "Sky Garden" referencing the sense that they appear to be floating in the air. The three spaces forming this garden are characterized as the "Cloud Sea Garden", the "Wind Wave Garden", and the "Cosmic River Garden" and are defined by traditional Japanese patterns created with different planting materials to create a modern Japanese style.

COMMENT

The existing 45 year old hotel's roof structural load bearing capacity of 60kg/m² presented a challenge during both design and implementation. Limited to a planting depth of only 10 cm our strategy was to keep the gardens simple, incorporating traditional patterns and materials such as stone in the creation of these modern gardens which are intended to be beautiful and easily understood when viewed from the hotel rooms above.

Tooru Miyakoda

"Waiting is an appreciation"

Rooftop Garden of Das Kurhaus

Landscape Architect: Jensen & Skodvin Arkitektkontor as
Client: HCC/Kappa
Location: Bad Gleichenberg, Austria
Site Area: 17, 500 m²
Cost: € 25,000, 000

CLIMATIC CONDITIONS

Austria's climate is mild and pleasant. There will be dry season in May to September and early October. April and November is the wet season, from later December to the march next year, it would be snow season for valley zone.

PLANTS

crassulaceae, maple kind of trees

EDITOR'S CHOICE

The roof of Das Kurhaus has been overlaid a vegetation insulation layer with selected sedum plants as groundcovers and gravel as perimeter enclosing. As a result, it will increase permeability and provide a 3D planting pattern on the roof, on which visitors feel as if in a park.

The project is situated in a protected park and consist of a treatment area with about 50 different rooms for medical treatments, a four star hotel with severaldifferent restaurants and cafes, and a public thermal bath for the patients andother guests.

The waiting areas in the middle of the treatment rooms for the patients are shaped around courtyards allowing sun and views to the trees, as to give the patients the impression of waiting in the park itself. A full treatment might last for several days and can consist of a number of different treatments, like different types of massages and baths in smaller private treatment rooms, a visit to a cold room with minus 110 degrees Celsius etc. Between these treatments the patients wait in the open and transparent waiting areas where the park is always close. One of the main aims of the architecture has been to un-institutionalize the architecture, make it resemble a hospital in as few ways as possible. The interior has been designed by an advertising bureau.

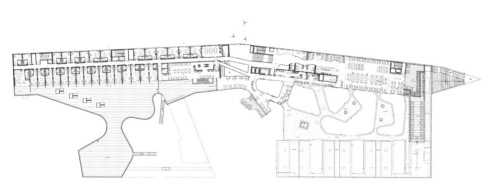

Site Plan

Roof Shape

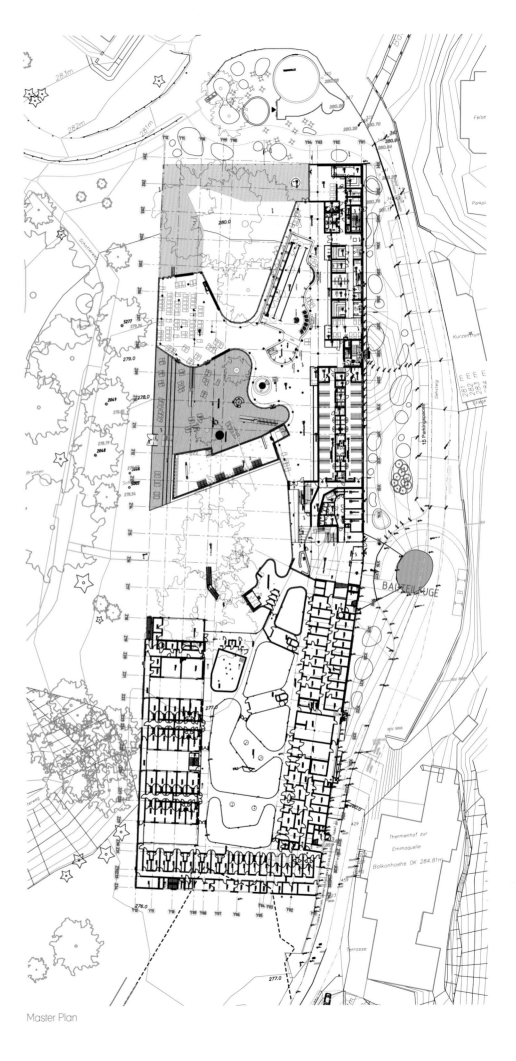

Master Plan

Architectural design according to its function is in three irregular layout. The first layer is the several seats of house connected each other, building on stilts in the central district in internal garden, and communicating with the treatment room by indoor corridor. The outer layer is the hotel area. The building layout is discrepancy in elevation. Level difference is three degree that is low, middle, and higher from outside to inside. The glass walls fall to the ground are all used in waiting area and corridor, making the person a very good visual environment, reducing boring feeling for waiting, person can also go out into atrium garden directly, enjoying the sun scenery when waiting. Crassulaceae plant is chose in atrium garden, matching with scattered maple kind of trees, to form the echo with difference building height. The tops of the buildings are covered by insulation layer, sticking with stonecrop plants, and with gravel to an edge to edge, these improved the water permeability, increased the roof vegetation pattern of the stereo feeling. the outermost layer of The building design on the top of hotel are single terraces, when standing here, to have an overlooking you can reach chain of mountains with visible green, a shadow of the trees flocking building. At nightfall, lights are born from glass walls fully, infiltrating wavering shadows of the trees, and the building is to serve as a foil to the dreaming.

Zhang Wenying

COMMENT

The purpose of Evidence-based design is to create a brand-new healthcare environment. The outdoor landscape as an important healthcare resource will help to reduce stress by rational use of natural factor, thus improve the overall heath sense of patients, visitors and staff. Relative to those without gardens, medical environment with gardens benefits in low cost and effective treatment to a certain extent. The park-like medical environment in the project has resulted in positive impact visually and psychologically and the application of Sedum plants greatly reduces maintenance costs.

Special thanks to the following invited experts and their exciting comments!

Zhang Wenying
Palm Landscape Architecture Planning Design Institute President

Song Sheng
A & I International (HK) Design Operational Manager
Landscape Architecture Center Manager

Farmerson
Farmerson Architects Design Director

Pang Wei
Beijing Turenscape Subdecanal
Guangzhou Turen Landscape Planning Co.,Ltd General Manager/ Chief Designer
The Graduate School of Landscape Architecture, Peking University Visiting Researcher
Guangzhou Academy of Fine Arts Visiting Professor

Lyndon Neri
Neri&Hu Design and Research Office Founding Partner

Rossana Hu
Neri&Hu Design and Research Office Founding Partner

Tooru Miyakoda
Keikan Sekkei Tokyo Co., Ltd President and Founder

Marion Weiss
Weiss / Manfredi Architecture / Landscape / Urbanism Cofounder
University of Pennsylvania Chair Professor of Architecture

Michael Manfredi
Weiss / Manfredi Architecture / Landscape / Urbanism Cofounder
Cornell University Visiting Professor

Paul Dracott
Paul Dracott Garden Design Garden Designer

Merilen Mentaal
Merilen Mentaal - MentaalLandscapes Garden Designer

David Kamp
Dirtworks Landscape Architecture, PC Garden Designer

Kim Mathews
Mathews Nielsen Landscape Architects Principal

Angie AU YEUNG
Designer

Special thanks to the following architects for their high-quality projects and nice supports!

Sawyer/Berson Architecture & Landscape Architecture, LLP

Balmori Associates

RSP Architects Planners & Engineers (Pte) Ltd

Arc Studio Architecture + Urbanism

Mathews Nielsen Landscape Architects

Jingsen Landscape Design Co., Ltd

Spurlock Poirier Landscape Architects

EARTHSCAPE

Liu Kuo Landscape Co., Ltd

JDS+BIG, EKJ

SWA Group

Hong Kong Drainage Services Department

HKSAR Government

KVR Arquitectura de Paisaje

Keikan Sekkei Tokyo Co., Ltd.

Jensen & Skodvin Arkitektkontor as

Patricia Fox MSGD / MBALI

Hoerr Schaudt Landscape Architects

Ken Smith Landscape Architect

Phillips Farevaag Smallenberg

T.R.O.P terrains+open space

Neri & Hu Design and Research Office

The Hong Kong Urban Renewal Authority

Sino Group

WEISS/MANFREDI Architecture/Landscape/Urbanism

Dominique Perrault Architecture

Andy Sturgeon Landscape and Garden Design

Secret Gardens of Sydney

Merilen Mentaal – MentaalLandscapes

Paul Dracott msgd

Nelson Byrd Woltz Landscape Architects

Jinny Blom Limited, Landscape Design

Terrain-NYC, Inc.

Dirtworks Landscape Architecture, PC

First Published in the United States

Gingko Press, Inc.
1321 Fifth Street
Berkeley, CA 94710

(510) 898-1195
(510) 898-1196

books@gingkopress.com
www.gingkopress.com

First published worldwide in 2013 by JTart Publishing & Media
Copyright © JTart Publishing & Media

Concept and compilation by HKASP
Graphic design by Meiguang Hou
Copy editing by Danielle Tsao

Printed in China
Size: 240mm×290mm
ISBN: 978-1-5842-3532-3
Price: $ 60

To find out about all of our publications, please visit www.jtart.com, or contact us via info@jtart.com.